Images of Victorian Hull

This book is dedicated to
Chris Ketchell (1944 – 2011)

F S Smith 1893

F S Smith's Drawings Volume 3

Contents

Research, compilation, design and publishing by
www.paul-gibson.com

ISBN 978-0-9568385-0-6

Printed by Dolman Scott Books www.dolman-scott.com

3 1929.62 (19 x 13.6 cm) First page An 1888 drawing,
looking south out of a court in Chapel Lane (see map on
page 42)

4 1961.98.3 (20 x 27.7 cm) Frontispiece A rare full colour
work dated 1893, showing the Anlaby Road looking west,
with the Convent of St Mary on the left (see map on page 82)

5 1929.226 (11.3 x 15.7 cm) Opposite page A scene
looking east across Sculcoates, showing the expansive
works of the Kingston Cotton Mills, and the former
Egginton's Oil Mill on the far left (see pages 34 and 35, and
map on page 22)

Foreword

Here, portrayed so vividly, are the streets and buildings of Hull just before a major period of re-development in the two decades before the First World War. There is not a wealth of topographical drawings or paintings of the city, so it was fortunate that Frederick Schultz Smith was encouraged from the early 1880s to record so prolifically the changing townscape. He produced hundreds of drawings, the majority of which are preserved in the collections of Hull Museums and Art Gallery.

In many cases Smith's drawings are the only record of buildings that are lost, particularly the more modest buildings in his street views. The subjects range from 17th Century almshouses, through Georgian terraces, to newly-built Board Schools and ornate commercial buildings. Most valuable are the scenes not captured then, or later by photographers, such as the jumble of industrial and domestic buildings along the Foredyke Stream, which provide a unique insight into an otherwise hidden aspect of the Victorian city.

There is a pleasing naivety about F S Smith's art. He was skilled in drawing buildings but little else, the almost Lowry-like simplicity of the out-of-scale figures and vehicles that parade along the streets, are part of the charm of these illustrations of a lost world.

This book is a welcome addition to the two previous volumes of F S Smith drawings, and to the growing literature on the history and buildings of Hull, much of it produced by those inspired by the late Chris Ketchell, including the author of this work, Paul Gibson. By his impressive output in print, and through his web-site and work with the Carnegie Heritage Centre, Paul has done much to advance our understanding of the lost heritage of the city. He is to be praised for the high standard of his productions, particularly The Anlaby Road, the two volumes of Hull – Then & Now, and now this publication. These have set a new bench-mark for such works in the quality of the reproduction, and content of the accompanying text.

David Neave

Introduction

The first book of F S Smith's work was published in 1989 and contained 122 of his drawings. A second volume – building on the success of the first – was released in 1990, and contained 135 drawings. Both proved to be very popular and were soon reprinted, but copies are now difficult to find. An exhibition of some of the Smith drawings was held at the Town Docks Museum (now the Hull Maritime Museum) from November 1990 until January 1991, cementing the public's interest and appreciation of his work. I only hope this third volume of over 140 of Smith's drawings proves as popular, and regenerates interest in this gifted artist. The views I have selected are formed into five chapters, covering the suburbs, as well as a short selection from the City centre and the Old Town. All of the images appear in print for the first time, with the exception of one or two that I feel will be better presented in this new format, than they were in the previous volumes. To add to their appreciation, the images are reproduced in full-colour, which will hopefully reflect their true appearance.

Carolyn Aldridge, a Hull Museums assistant specialising in Social History, compiled the text for the first volume, and Hull's foremost local historian Chris Ketchell compiled the text for the second. At that time genealogical research was not as hugely popular as it is now, and the vast resources that we enjoy today – mostly Internet based – were then unavailable. Consequently, the version of Smith's family history that was given was slightly speculative in some areas. Happily, with all of the resources that are now available, I have been able to conduct further detailed research into his family history, and present a fuller and more precise picture of Smith's life and family background.

Frederick Schultz Smith

Edward Smith, a journeyman watchmaker by trade, came to Hull from his birthplace of Liverpool during the 1840s. By 1848, then aged 25, he was recorded in a trade directory of that year living in King Street off the east side of Charles Street. It appears that whilst living here he met 19 years old Maria Cape, possibly whilst a resident in her house, as she – or her mother, as both were called Maria – kept a lodging-house at no.20 King Street. Both mother and daughter were listed there in the 1841 Census, and their lodging house was still listed in the 1848 trade directory.

On the 12 April 1849 Edward and Maria were married, at the Parish Church of Sculcoates – St Mary's Bankside. Maria was listed as a spinster in the marriage records, Edward's father Henry David Smith was noted as a musician, and Maria's father Leonard Cape as a master mariner. By the time of the 1851 Census, newly married Edward and Maria Smith had moved south to London, and were living at no.14 Lascelles Place in Finsbury.

Edward was noted in the census as a 28 years old 'watchmaker-finisher', with his wife – then aged 21 years. By 1854 they had moved to the Sussex coast, where they were recorded in the next census in 1861. The couple had become a family whilst still in Finsbury, with the birth of their first daughter Annie, but were now living at no.16 Warwick Place in Worthing, a pleasant area just a stone's-throw from the seafront. Warwick Place is shown top-left (previous page) in a 1970s photograph, and below that is Frederick Smith's birthplace as it appears today.

Edward was still listed as a watchmaker in the 1861 Census, although his age was recorded as 33 years – when he should have been at least 38 – a common occurrence in an time when people were less conscious of their birthdays. Maria was by then 30 years old, and as well as mother to Annie E Smith, aged seven years (born in London), they had a new baby boy named Frederick Schultz Smith. Frederick was born at no.16 Warwick Place, Worthing on 25 May 1859, and the birth was registered on 5 July 1859. Why his parents chose Schultz as his middle name, is unclear, although several Schultz' lived in the King Street area in the 1850s – including female members in the same trade as his mother Maria, and of a similar age; it is possible that they were close family friends.

The family moved back to Maria's hometown of Hull by 1862, where they had another child who they named Florence, born in that year. The family are recorded in the 1871 Census at no.22 or 24 Myton Street – often recorded as Little Anne Street at this north end – and this may just have been rented rooms in a lodging house. Sometime before the 1871 Census Maria had sadly died, and Edward was listed as a 39 years old widower, and still a watchmaker. Annie – the eldest daughter, was a 16 years old 'domestic servant', nine years old Florence was a scholar, and Frederick – by then recorded as 11 years old – was also a scholar, his birthplace erroneously recorded as Hull. By the time of the 1881 Census the family were still living at the north end of Myton Street, where Edward was still listed as a watchmaker, and his two daughters were noted as servants, although Florence was unemployed. Probably struggling to make ends meet, and living in poor surroundings, the family were no doubt reliant not just upon Edward's wage, but also that of young Frederick, by then aged around 22 and listed as a clerk.

Kelly's 1885 directory records that Edward Smith was by then a commission agent, resident at no.2 Rose Street – a newly built street within the Swann Estate, at the north end of Waterloo Street. Rose Street ran between Seaton Street and Symons Street, and no.2 was the first house on the south side – near the entrance to Fern Terrace. The photograph top-right dates from 1971, and shows similar houses in Rose Street, adjacent to the Smith's home. Rose Street must have been a huge improvement from the Myton Street property for the family, who were to remain there for almost 30 years. The 1891 Census listed Edward

as a 61 years old draughtsman, with his two daughters still at home; Annie as a 31 years old domestic servant 'out of place' (unemployed), and Florence as a 23 years old housekeeper for the family. The young Frederick meanwhile, was listed as an 'architectural artist', and would have been 32 years old, although his age was recorded as just 27. Between 1893 and 1896 Edward Smith died, leaving Frederick as the head of the household; he was first recorded in the trade directories as an artist from that address in an 1895 directory. This must have been a difficult time for Frederick, as his patron Mr Fewster had also passed away in 1896 (see later).

The 1901 Census records Frederick S. Smith, as a 37 years old 'pen and pencil artist and sculptor' – 'living on his own account' at home (although he was probably nearer 41 by that time). His sister Florence, recorded as 36 years old, was still single and remained the 'domestic housekeeper', but sister Annie's whereabouts from the 1890s onwards are unknown. Fred and Florence remained at no.2 Rose Street until at least 1913, and just after the First World War ended, Frederick and his sister moved east to a small terrace off Arundel Street, Holderness Road. No.2 Eastbourne Avenue was another small working class terraced house, but at least had the benefit of a small front garden (see photographs of the terrace and Smith's home on page 6). Smith and his spinster sister remained there until his untimely death.

Another local artist – Eric Abbot – who was a friend of Smith in his later years, recalled that although too old to be called up for service, Smith had supported the views of the conscientious objectors. Eric also suggested that Smith had left Hull during the war years, when the anti-German riots took place in Hull, spurred on by the Zeppelin bombings in 1915. Having a Germanic middle name, would no doubt have only added to Frederick's troubles. This account from Mr Abbot would also explain why

Smith was not listed in any local trade directories during the years of the First World War, and returned after the war to a different address.

Frederick Schultz Smith died of complications brought on by cancer of the stomach in the old Hull Royal Infirmary in Prospect Street, on 26 September 1925, aged 66; his sister Florence was present at the death. He was buried on 30 September 1925 in the Hull General Cemetery on Spring Bank West, following a service at St Andrew's Church Holderness Road. Mourners at the burial included his sister, librarian W G B Page, and many neighbours and friends. His grave now lies apparently unmarked and overgrown, any memorial seemingly lost.

Frederick Schultz Smith's Art

Coming from such an apparently humble background, it is difficult to see how Smith acquired his artistic talent, which presumably was just a natural gift. His father may have had some artistic leaning however, by the nature of his work as a watchmaker, and later as a draughtsman. Living in Myton Street in the late 1860s and early 1870s, it is likely that Frederick would have attended South Myton (Adelaide Street) School, although several reports in the local newspapers after his death suggest he had art school training. The Hull Daily Mail of 1 October 1925, reported that his talent was encouraged by the vicar of St Mary's Church, Bankside (the Reverend W J Pearson) – who allegedly paid the first term's fees for Smith so that he might study at the Hull School of Art, and gave him his first commission for a drawing of the interior of St Mary's Church in Bankside. Other reports also confirmed that he studied under Mr Menzies – art master at the Hull School of Art, although a conflicting report in the Hull Times of 3 October 1925, noted that Smith:

> '... had no School of Art training, but he had a natural gift'.

Newspaper reports during the 1880s record many events and exhibitions at the Hull School of Art, but none appear to list Smith amongst the exhibiting or awarded pupils. Some of the reports note that several regular patrons of the school, often donated prizes for the best students. Amongst these were one-time mayor of Hull Mr (later Sir) Albert K Rollit, and more notably – Charles E Fewster (1847-1896), who was a partner in local paint manufacturing company Thomas Fewster & Son, and also a town councillor. If Smith did attend the School of Art – it is possible that it was there that he came to the attention of Mr Fewster.

Charles Fewster was a noted collector of all things local, including coins and tokens, books, directories, guides, manuscripts, and notably – maps and topographical views. Whatever the circumstances were, it is from around 1880 that Fewster first employed Frederick Schultz Smith – then around 21 years of age – to record those parts of Hull that were being demolished or redeveloped. Hull was in the middle of a great upheaval of 'City improvements' that took place from the 1880s, which continued into the early 1900s. In employing Smith in this way, he was to instigate the compilation of a unique visual record of many Hull buildings that would otherwise have gone without record.

The majority of Smith's surviving works consequently date from the 1880s and early 1890s, with the occasional work from as early as 1880. It is the early 1880s drawings that are the best executed, and most detailed. Smith was left-handed, and worked mostly in pen and ink, later using washes to fill in. Several colour watercolours also exist (see frontispiece), including many of nearby towns and villages. His drawings vary in size but are mostly much smaller than one would expect. This is all the more remarkable, when one examines the fine detail that Smith managed to compress within his many sketches. Thomas Sheppard, the long-time Director of Hull Museums, writing of Smith in 1929, noted that he was a:

'... well-known character, for many years familiar in doorways and sheltered places, sketching with his left hand with lightning rapidity. From an artistic point of view his works are of exceptional merit, but quite apart from this, the amount of microscopic detail he put into them was remarkable'.

Several small and incomplete, rough pencil drawings survive that suggest he completed some works at home, from sketches made on the spot. Many of the images used in this book, are presented larger than the actual size of the originals, although I have also listed the original dimensions within the captions for reference.

Smith may have begun his local drawings at an early age, before Mr Fewster intervened, as a picture reproduced in the Hull Times of 8 June 1935 was supposedly 'drawn when he was 13 years old' (1872). A later article in the Hull Times of 16 August 1890 noted:

'Mr F S Smith, artist, shows a good selection of sketches and water colour drawings, amongst which, especially worthy of merit may be mentioned a fine pencil sketch of 'The Land o' Green Ginger', showing the tower of Holy Trinity Church in the distance, a picture which presents much evidence of careful study and painstaking execution. Several other exceedingly pretty little sketches are deserving of notice, particularly a study of Beverley Market-place in sepia and a neat little watercolour sketch of the Hull Market-place and King William Statue; also sketches of Ottringham and Ferriby Churches, and a well executed picture of the Anlaby-road, showing the Convent and St Matthew's Church. We understand the artist is engaged at present on a large picture of the interior of Holy Trinity Church, which is approaching completion and shows considerable promise of being a very fine work'.

SPRING STREET

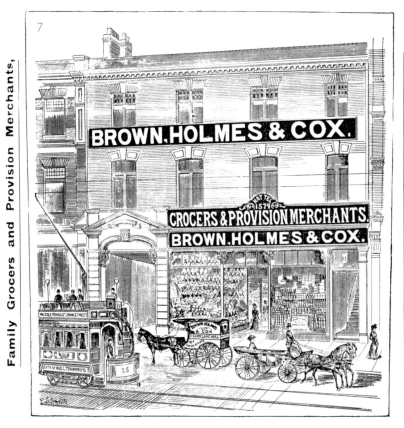

Some of BROWN, HOLMES & COX'S Winter SPECIALITIES

WILL BE

SMOKED RUSSIAN OX-TONGUES & UNPRESSED RIGA CAVIARE.

SEASON COMMENCES END OF NOVEMBER.

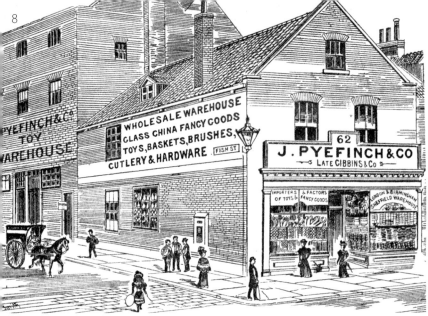

His commissioned work on behalf of Mr Fewster, probably ended with his patron's death in 1896, or even earlier. Smith continued to earn a living – however small – as a sculptor, and by creating drawings for use in books and newspapers, as well as creating views of individual properties and shops for use in advertising, such as those shown here. From 1894-96 he produced a series of drawings for the Hull News, showing 'Views of Holderness', and from 3 April 1900 to 13 April 1901 – a series named 'Holderness Illustrated'. Another series of drawings was published from 27 April to 31 August 1901, and was entitled 'East Riding Illustrated'.

An obituary noted that he was a 'familiar figure in the city', and was 'wholly indifferent to the attention he was arousing' whilst making his drawings. Eric Abbot confirmed that as Smith sketched away, he could be oblivious to the small crowd gathered behind him, until he stepped back when his work was done. Eric recalled him clearly as a tall man, always immaculately dressed, touring the city making his drawings, staying out from early morning until the evening, and always with his attache case. Within the case were his drawing board and drawing materials, and a telescopic easel – not unlike a music stand. Dressed in a stiff-collared shirt, and wearing a long overcoat and bowler hat, Smith was very businessman-like in appearance, according to Mr Abbot. Sadly, there are as yet no known images of Frederick Schultz Smith.

Many of his later drawings were unsigned, but can usually be identified as his work. More sizeable works hung in the Guildhall and many offices and corridors of the Corporation, whilst others remained in private collections – some only seeing the light of day in recent years, when they appear in local auctions and sales. The apparent decline in his output, and the lessening demand for his work, may in part be linked to the increasing

use of photography in advertising, and indeed in general use. The picture-postcard craze that gripped the country from the early 1900s, provided a much more affordable, accurate and almost instant representation of the Edwardian world, and one that could be posted cheaply. From c.1900 the quality of his work is noticeably different and less detailed, possibly as a result of failing eyesight. His surviving drawings from after 1900, when he would have been around 40 years of age, are predominantly of a larger size. He continued to work until just before his death, his final drawings often depicting scenes in the city centre, which had changed so very much during his lifetime. In 1925 he made drawings of King Edward Street and Queen Victoria Square, and was seen drawing in Manor Street only days before being admitted to the hospital.

Some years after the death of councillor Fewster in 1896, his widow and daughter kindly donated almost 300 examples of Smith's work to the City, which form the basis of the Hull Museums collection. These have been supplemented with others over the years, and the collection forms an invaluable resource for the people of Hull. Outdoor, topographical and architectural photography, was still fairly unusual in the 1880s and 1890s. Consequently, the images that Frederick Schultz Smith created, provide a fairly accurate picture of our City and the surrounding villages, from a period that we would otherwise have little or no visual record of. Hopefully, this third volume of drawings will regenerate interest and public awareness, in the work of one of our most prolific and talented artists. The F S Smith collection is one of the most important held by Hull Museums, and the Hull History Centre. A long-overdue new exhibition of his drawings, is to be held at the Hull Maritime Museum, from 9 May until 11 September 2011.

Paul Gibson

1 East Hull

9 Chapter title page 1929.362 (12.2 x 16.6 cm) The Corporation had rejected the idea of a refuse destructor for several years, until finally approving it in 1882. The chimneys central to this drawing, mark the site of the Chapman Street Refuse Destructor, built on the site of a former flax and cotton mill. Costing just under £8,000 – including the land – it burnt every item of collected waste, except night-soil. Completed in December 1882, it began work immediately, its furnaces raging 24 hours a day – every day. In 1882 just as in 2011 however, no-one wanted the destructor on their doorstep, and protests against the destructor and its location continued for many months. Despite this, it was a huge success, and remained in use for over a century. Demolished in 1984, the site is now the location for the '2 Wheel Centre' – part of a Council youth development service. Smith however, was probably recording a new bridge over the Holderness Drain, constructed c.1888 to replace an old wooden structure. The bridge was demolished in the 1970s, and is now the site of a mini-roundabout.

10 1929.375 (10 x 14.2 cm) above A point further south along the Holderness – or Sutton Drain – than the previous image. The church tower in the far distance is St Peter's in Drypool, which was badly damaged during the Second World War and demolished, and the footbridge in the centre marks the point at which St Mark Street crossed the stream. Originally a toll bridge, this original structure was also replaced with a more substantial road bridge c.1888.
On the right is one of the original gasometers of the Sutton, Southcoates & Drypool Gasworks, established in Sitwell Street in 1847. A later gasometer dating from c.1896 remains – west of the one shown, and the tall chimneys, are still clearly visible on the ground.
The drain was culverted in the 1960s, but its route can still be seen, and a pleasant cycle track and foot path follow its alignment from this point, continuing north for several miles.

Sponsored by Geoff Percival

11 1981.415.59 (11 x 15.6 cm) Smith appears to have produced very few images of East Hull, and the majority of his surviving works depict mostly central and western views. This December 1889 drawing, shows hoardings around a corner site announcing a 'Christmas Treat', and 'P. T. Barnum's Greatest Show on Earth'. Looking south along Dansom Lane, on the right is the entrance to St Mark Street, and on the left the entrance to one of Hull's lost streets – Wilde Street – all trace of which is lost, beneath Reckitt Benckiser's huge complex.

Dansom Lane, originally known as Clow Lane, was also referred to as Mill Lane, as three windmills were established here during the early 19th Century, two of which survived at the time Smith made his sketch. From the 1820s however, Clow or Mill Lane, was mostly referred to as Dansom Lane.

The most northerly of the three mills was Turner's Whitening Mill, situated south of Chapman Street, off the right of this picture. This was demolished by Reckitt's and is now the location of their 'court of honour', where staff who fought in the First World War are remembered. In the distance are the remains of Dale's Flour Mill, built c.1803, and in the foreground the elegant five-sail Subscription Mill. Subscription Mill, another corn mill, was founded in 1801 and was still in use at the time of Smith's drawing. It too was demolished by Reckitt's for their well-known Brasso building at the turn of the century.

To the right of the picture, on the corner of St Mark Street, was the shop of grocer Harry Branton at no.51 Dansom Lane, which also served as an off-licence.

12 1929.148 (11.2 x 15.8 cm) Only three buildings survive from this view showing the entrance to the Holderness Road, which Smith dated 1888. On the left, at the corner of Dansom Lane and marked by a flagpole, is the Holderness Hotel – established c.1834 and re-fronted in 1914, in the more familiar imitation half-timbered style. On the opposite corner of Dansom Lane is the wonderful c.1850 curved frontage of no.1 Holderness Road – currently a kitchen and bathroom showroom – but shown in Smith's sketch as Dickens Brothers grocers shop, with a pillar letter box on the corner. The pillar letter box was removed shortly after this sketch was made, when a post office was established within Fox's chemist shop on the left of the picture. Next door to the Holderness Hotel, shown with an open awning, was the butchers' shop of John Thompson.

The other surviving building, is the school room of the former Holderness Road Presbyterian Church – the smaller of the two distant buildings (see page 16). The long terrace on the right contains the oldest buildings within the scene, including the low-houses built around the unusual octagonal base of the Blockhouse Mill. The mill appears on Jeffrey's 1775 plan of Hull, suggesting these small buildings – typical of houses in the Drypool area – were also of that date. These buildings and many others, were demolished during the construction of Clarence Street from c.1898, although parts of the Blockhouse Mill survived into the 1960s. At the time of Smith's drawing, the arched entrance on the far right marked cab proprietor Edward Annison's premises. The Annison family were well-known in Hull as coach builders, and latterly funeral directors based in Witham.

Sponsored by the Hull Maritime Society

13 1929.146 (11 x 15.7 cm) In 2011 the front doors of the former Waterloo Tavern (presently closed), still open onto the remains of Harcourt Street, which still has a section of granite-sett road, flagged footpath, and a Victorian tiled street name on the pub's front wall. Known locally as the Bush, the Waterloo was established c.1815, the name possibly inspired by Wellington's victory at Waterloo that year. Looking north along Harcourt Street, the Waterloo was situated at the far end of the street, occupying the last block of property on the right hand side, in this c.1882 view. Buildings on the east side of Great Union Street are visible in the distance, and the line of buildings along the east (right) side of Harcourt Street were mostly Georgian. Some of these houses dated from the 1770s, and possibly earlier, although the street was only laid-out and named from c.1800. The pub was re-built in 1932, as we see it today, but what other buildings that remained in Harcourt Street were demolished following Blitz damage sustained during the Second World War. The street remained open to traffic following the war, until the Clarence Flour Mills (also Blitz damaged) were re-built in 1952, and extended across the site of the old street during the 1950s.

At the time of the 1881 Census – just before Smith drew this sketch, 15 of the 16 houses in the street were occupied, and at least 103 people were resident.

All but two of the houses had at least one occupant that worked in trades associated with the river, ship-building, or the timber industry – including a lath render, ship's carpenter, wood sawyer, and a keel-man. The larger property at the far right, was the business premises of 39 years old William Salmon (formerly of Salmon & Armit), who was a mast and block maker. His offices were empty on the evening of the census, as he was at his private residence at 16 Beaumont Street.

14 1929.147 (8.5 x 11 cm) In the distance of image 12 (on page 13) is a terrace with small front gardens, alongside the Presbyterian Church. This was known as Somerstown, when built in a piecemeal fashion from c.1820, although the original layout included a gap part way along the terrace, that was filled with a later three-storey building. This may account for the ghostly way in which Smith drew the property on the far right of the terrace, which may have been constructed or re-built at the time he made the sketch.

Now nos.38 to 50 Holderness Road, Somerstown ends here, at the entrance to Williamson Street shown on the left. The iron railings enclosing the small front areas, were removed from the late 19th Century, as the houses were gradually converted into shops. Smith made this sketch c.1883, at which time the two end properties were occupied by surgeon William Holder at the corner, and coal merchant Frederick Lord next door. At the time of writing these two houses have been amalgamated into one property, known as Muttley's Motorcycles. It is hard to relate the present busy commercial properties of Somerstown, which survives in full in 2011, to the quiet and private housing that Smith drew portrayed.

On the far right of the picture, the brick pillar marks the boundary of more up-market houses in Wilton Terrace, part of a matching pair of properties, which remain – either side of the entrance to Wilton Street – on the north side of the Holderness Road.

F.S.Smith

15 1929.143 (11.5 x 15.4 cm) The houses in the Somerstown terrace can just be glimpsed in the centre of this c.1884 view of the Holderness Road, looking west, back towards the city centre. On the far left the iron railings and young trees, mark the front of a large garden of a detached house on the corner of Field Street, that was latterly the home of the Vicar of Drypool. The East Hull Liberal Club was built upon this site around 1887, and it is now the site of a second hand car dealer. This was to be the fate of many of Hull's lost churches and chapels. Beyond Field Street are a few remaining properties in East Parade, another long terrace similar to Somerstown. In the centre of East Parade can be seen the Holderness Road Presbyterian Church of 1874, that was badly damaged during the Second World War. The church was demolished in 1972, but the adjoining schoolroom remains, latterly the site of a bowling alley and the Green Man pub. On the far right 'provision dealer' Harry Coulson's shop stands on the corner of Bright Street, which was laid out in 1875. Beyond Bright Street is the frontage of the Holderness Road Primitive Methodist Chapel, which opened in 1864. This neighbourhood, like many of the major roads throughout Hull, contained many large and often ornate churches and chapels, almost all now gone without trace. The Bright Street chapel too was damaged in the Second World War, and demolished in 1960, and the plot was also the location of another car showroom until very recently.

F.S. Smith
1889

16 1929.241 (13.3 x 18.9 cm) Shown here in 1889 is Williamson Street, looking north towards the Holderness Road, near the entrance to Abbey Street on the right. Williamson Street was developed during the 1830s, and in June 1838 building plots were still being offered for sale in the Hull Advertiser: 'Upwards of sixty lots of most desirable building ground situate in Williamson-street, and the adjacent new streets in the townships of Southcoates and Drypool, and in the immediate vicinity of the Holderness Turnpike Road and the Hull and Hedon New Turnpike Road. The ground, which is an open and airy, and healthful situation, and within fifteen minutes' walk of the centre of the Town of Hull, is suitable for the erection of respectable Dwelling Houses, with Gardens'.

Williamson Street was soon developed with dwelling houses, a school, two churches, shops and industrial premises such as the Holderness Iron Foundry - the chimney of which can be seen in the distance on the left.
The ornate Gothic tower and spire of the Latimer Congregational chapel can be seen on the left, designed by Samuel Musgrave. The church was established in 1869, in a temporary building, but this red-brick building was built in 1874. Both of Williamson Street's churches, the other being the Henry Hodge Memorial Primitive Methodist Chapel, were demolished in the 1960s. The only original buildings that survive in the street, are industrial buildings at the north end, and a cluster of housing including the terrace 'Myrtle Avenue', on the east side.

17 1929.299 (13.3 x 19.2 cm) left The Kingston upon Hull School Board was established in 1871, following the Education Act of 1870. Under the presidency of Sir Henry Cooper, the first schools to be built were announced as Courtney Street, Lincoln Street, and this one in Williamson Street, which replaced the Holderness Ward School. Tenders were invited to build the Williamson Street school in 1874, and the contract was awarded to builder A W Stanley of Midland Street. The school, built to the designs of the School Board's architect and surveyor William Botterill, was still under construction in January 1875. The first schoolmistress was Christiania Jackson of Saltaire, who was first appointed in December 1873 and was to be paid £70 per annum.

The school provided 750 places in separate boys, girls, and infants departments, and a separate junior department was added in 1894. This increased the accommodation to 1,010 places and the average attendance was 934 in 1904. The boys department closed in 1908, the girls in 1932, leaving just the junior mixed and infants departments, which were amalgamated in 1940. The school closed c.1980 and was used latterly by Abbey Industries, as a Youth Training Centre before closure and demolition in 1993.

18 1929.298 (13.6 x 19.5 cm) right
Chapman Street Board school was built in 1885, just four years before Smith made his sketch. Note the original narrow width of Cleveland Street (then Wilmington Lane at this point), which runs left to right across the picture, with Chapman Street itself leading off partly in shadow to the right. Originally known as Albert Street, the name was changed to Chapman Street in September 1862, after William Chapman a member of the local board of health. Initial accommodation was for 866 pupils, but a junior block added in 1902 increased the accommodation to 1,163 – comprising of 310 boys, 310 girls, 300 juniors, and 243 infants. The average attendance fell from 951 in 1904 to 552 in 1938, due in part to the slum clearance programmes that had begun in this area in the early 1930s. The junior department closed following Second World War damage in 1941, but mixed all-age boys and girls departments, and an infants department remained in use.

The school closed in 1979, following the demolition of most of the remaining housing in the immediate area. The building was later used as an annexe of the Hull College of Further Education for a short time, and was demolished in 1991.

19 1929.297 (13 x 18.9 cm) left Courtney Street Board School was built – as the date stone confirms – in 1873, the second of the School Board's new schools to be built in Hull (there were 14 by 1879). Tenders for its construction were still being advertised in the local press in January 1873, to be submitted by the end of February – so the school must have been completed very late in the year. The school actually opened in 1874, built at a cost of £6,546, and with accommodation for 816 pupils; the first staff were school master Mr Thomas Broad, school mistress Miss Mary Spaven, and the fittingly named Miss Mary Little was the infants mistress. Smith made his drawing of the buildings, located on the west side of the street – at the Holderness Road end – in 1887.

A junior department was added in 1895, and other alterations enlarged the overall accommodation to 1,071 – being 296 boys, 296 girls, 206 juniors, and 273 infants. Average attendance was 962 in 1904, and 758 in 1938. The junior department closed following damage sustained during the Second World War, reducing the provision to just an all-age boys and girls department, and an infants. Probably another victim of the compulsory purchase orders that cleared away swathes of housing during the 1960s and 1970s, the school closed c.1971 and was demolished soon after.

20 1929.305 (13.5 x 19 cm) right Smith dated his drawing of Crowle Street Board School December 1889, just five years after its construction in 1884. Plans of the proposed school were first shown to the board in 1882, and tenders were invited for the building works in September of that year. In 1883 a loan of £8,924 was taken from the Hull Savings Bank for the purchase of the site and erection of the school, at a rate of four percent per annum. Hockney & Liggins of Witham and Great Union Street were appointed as builders, with costs of £5,500, and the site cost £2,427. Mr Hockney lived at no.7 Somerstown – mentioned on page 15. A further £250 was allocated for internal fittings, £250 for heating, and £250 for the surveyor's fees and clerk of work's salary. Initial accommodation was for 796 pupils, and a new junior block, built in 1897, increased this figure to 1,072. This was later reduced to 1,036 (266 boys, 266 girls, 261 mixed juniors, and 243 infants). Average attendance was 1,001 in 1911, and 768 by 1938. The senior boys and girls departments were transferred to Craven High School in 1945, leaving a combined junior and infant school. The main buildings in Crowle Street were demolished in 1996, although the 1897 extension survives at the rear of the site, in Churchill Street. In its final years the main building was used as an annexe of the Hull College of Further Education.

21 1929.396 (12.1 x 16.5 cm) The caption for this drawing notes that it depicts 'Alexandra Dock, nearing completion, May 1883'. Smith's vantage point was the south-west corner of the dock. On the left and right, transit sheds are in the course of construction, and in the middle-distance on the right is the lock entrance to the dock, with the metal swing-bridge in an open position. On the left – beyond the West Jetty and the scaffolding – can be seen the tower of the Hedon Road Prison, and beyond that the tower of the crematorium and the top of the crematorium chapel. Note the two figures, placed in the dock for scale. The Hull, Barnsley & West Riding Junction Railway & Dock Co, officially opened the Alexandra Dock in July 1885. Initially it had 46.5 acres of water space, 160 acres of quayage, two miles length of quays, and two large graving docks. Amongst other things, the attraction of vessels of an ordinary draught being able to enter the dock at any state of the tide, meant it was a huge success. It was also the first fully hydraulically-operated dock in the country, and several original hydraulic pumping station buildings survive on the dock – now listed buildings. An original 100 ton-lift steam crane, situated at the east end of the dock, was given grade two-star Listed Building status in 1990, along with the dock walls, lock-gates, graving docks, and the 17-acre extension dock of 1899. Alexandra Dock closed in 1982, but re-opened in 1991, and remains extremely successful, mostly due to Hull's continuing strong links with the timber trade.

2 Sculcoates

22 Chapter title page 1929.231 (11.3 x 15.8 cm) Elm Tree House – central to this view – was the home of tanner Benjamin Casson, who built the house in the late 1840s, opposite the east end of Harley Street – and just south of Providence Row. Looking north, the view includes the rear of houses in Waterloo Street on the right. Through the gate in the fence on the left, was the eastern bank of the Cottingham Drain, and in the distance can be seen the chimney of the Stepney Paper Mill, and the tower of a property on the Beverley Road.
When Smith made this sketch in 1883, he was no doubt recording the scene as the land here was about to be built upon, when Holmes Street was laid-out later in the 1880s (see page 30).

23 1929.373 (11.3 x 15.6 cm) above The two boys are fishing in the Cottingham Drain, which runs east towards its outfall into the River Hull, in this early 1880s view. Smith was facing west when he made the drawing, with Richmond Terrace on his right, bisected by the entrance to Waterloo Street – marked by the drain bridge and the flagpole of the Burns Head pub. On the left was Cottingham Place, bisected by Charles Street, which ended at the same bridge. At the end of Richmond Terrace was the former Ragged & Industrial School, built in 1856 to the designs of William Botterill. The chimneys, and the ventilator cowls mark the rear of Moors' & Robson's Crown Brewery, established in Raywell Street by Henry Moor c.1848. Taken over by Hewitt's in 1960, the last brew here was made in 1964.

24 1929.313 (11.6 x 15.5 cm) above, and
25 1929.222 (12.2 x 9.6 cm) left Two views
showing St Paul's Street made from slightly
different vantage points, but both looking south
towards the junction with Liddell Street on the
far right, and Cannon Street on the left.
St Paul's Anglican church, designed by William
Hey Dykes of York, was consecrated on 20
October 1847. The church was demolished
in 1976, but a new church remains in use on
the site, as does the old vicarage. St Paul's
Street was laid out in the early 1850s but not
built upon until 1857, when St Paul's National
school (see above) was built to the north of the
church. Designed by William Botterill in the early
English style, the Hull Packet reported that the
school was initially for boys only, with just two
classrooms catering for 'upwards of 300 children'.
In the centre of the larger view is the East Riding
Hotel, established c.1867, which survives in its
re-fronted form. In the distance – the tower of
Christ Church in Worship Street, and several
large chimneys apparently under construction
or repair, in the Scott Street area. Despite severe
damage in the Second World War, and having
been cleared of most of its housing in 1959, St
Paul's Street remains in part, although re-named
at this south end – and rebuilt at the north.

26 1929.254 (13.2 x 19 cm) St Paul's Church was built of distinctive rough stone, brought from Brough by contractors Simpson & Malone. Its tower and spire were added later, forming a bold focal point at the corner of Cannon Street and the later St Paul's Street. This 1888 drawing shows Cannon Street looking west towards the junction with St Paul's Street. Cannon Street was laid-out running west from the junction of Green Lane and Lockwood Street, and originally went only as far as the entrance to Gibson Street, shown on the right. Laid out in 1800, Gibson Street was named after stonemason Michael Gibson, who built the original large houses in the street. Gibson Street was often known as Boteler Street at this south end, reverting to Gibson Street later in the 19th Century. Cannon Street had four pubs in its heyday; the East Riding Hotel, the Salutation Inn, the Sow & Pigs, and the Red Lion.

Situated at the corner of Gibson Street, and marked by a gas-lamp in Smith's drawing, the Red Lion was established c.1872. Initially owned by Kendall & Gruby's Exchange Brewery, it survived until 1972, when the street was cleared of its housing and shops under a Compulsory Purchase Order. Alongside the Red Lion were two houses, and then the premises of undertaker George Broughton, and hairdresser Charles Walter Eastwood – complete with barber's pole.
On the left (south) side of the street was the entrance to the 'Old Foundry' of the engineering company Rose, Downs & Thompson. Beyond the entrance are shops – including Terry's newsagent – interspersed by the entrances to several tiny enclosed courts known as Johnson's Place, Providence Place, and Elizabeth's Place. Also on the left, was the entrance to Cannon Place, built when the Old Foundry was first established c.1777.

27 1929.171 (13.3 x 19.1 cm) below, and 28 1929.302 (13.4 x 18.9 cm) right
Two views of Lincoln Street, both dated 1888; the larger image was made from
the junction with Swann Street, looking south towards the raised footpath at
High Flags on Wincolmlee, shown in the distance. Although not mentioned in the
trade directories until the 1820s, Lincoln Street was named much earlier.
One of the first buildings to be built in the street was a six horse-power, steam-
powered corn mill – noted in the Hull Packet of 27 December 1814, as 'newly
erected in Lincoln Street'. Lincoln Street was extended north across the Prince
Albert Strawberry Gardens from c.1860. On the left, was the Samuel Hodge
Memorial Primitive Methodist Chapel, built in 1872 at a cost of £5,300. Closing in
1935, the site was mostly cleared, although parts remained until the street was
cleared in a 1966 Compulsory Purchase Order. On the right (west) side of the
street, was the Lincoln Street Board School (shown right). Opened in 1873, it was
one of the first newly-built Board Schools to open, and was demolished in 1997.

29 1929.316 (10 x 12.3 cm) left An undated Smith drawing, probably made in the early 1880s, showing Blundell Street Board School. Blundell Street school opened in 1878. Catering initially for 750 pupils, it later had 278 boys, 273 girls, and 246 infants.

Following Second World War Blitz damage, it was reduced to a junior mixed school, and closed in the 1970s. Latterly it was home to the Hull School of Architecture and The Strand – a student union venue that regularly held live music. After finally closing in 1998, it fell victim to the first in a series of fires in 1999, which have in part reduced it to a derelict shell.

Now the oldest survivor of Hull's original 37 Board Schools, and a Grade Two Listed Building, hopefully a new use will soon be found for the former Blundell Street School, and prevent what would be the sad loss of a damaged but nonetheless historic building.

The alignment of Blundell Street itself partially survives as an access road to the site of the old school, now mostly enveloped by a former car parking area, and re-named with this west end of Brunswick Avenue, as Strand Close.

30 1929.304 (13.5 x 19.3 cm) right

Clifton Street Board School, in a drawing Smith dated 1889. Clifton Street was laid out in the early 1870s, as part of a huge swathe of residential developments, stretching from the Cottingham Drain as far north as Fountain Road. Clifton Street and Blundell Street formed part of a section developed as the 'Brunswick Estate', situated around Brunswick House on the Beverley Road – the home of Henry Blundell (see pages 62-63).

Clifton Street Board School was built in 1889, at the north end of Clifton Street, with its back to the Cottingham Drain. Initial accommodation was for 250 boys, 252 girls, and 276 infants.

Average attendance was 761 in 1904, which reduced to 601 in 1938. One of very few surviving original Board Schools still in use, it is now known as the Clifton Primary School – its address now Burslem Street, although the alignment of Clifton Street remains. It now has an average of 150 pupils, and remains very popular.

F.S.Smith

31 1929.374 (11.3 x 15.5 cm) Designed by J Fox Sharpe, the local Board of Health's engineer and surveyor, Sculcoates Bridge opened in January 1875, the culmination of planning that began in 1869. Spanning the river from Chapman Street in the east, to Swann Street in the west (on the left of the drawing), the bridge provided an essential link between the industrial areas of Wilmington and the Groves, and Sculcoates. It also saw an end to the 'Brewhouse Wrack', a dangerous, ramshackle workers ferry that operated during the 19th Century. Built at a cost of less than £18,000, this was only the second public bridge over the River Hull, and is now Hull's oldest surviving original bridge. The wheel on the right of the picture was used to open the bridge, which was initially by hand power alone, using machinery geared into a fixed rack that is still visible today.

The man depicted on the boat, was probably pushing on the bridge as it was about to be opened, helping it glide northwards to its open resting point. A bridge across the River Hull, south of the present North Bridge, existed in the 14th Century, and possibly earlier. This was the first bridge over the River Hull, and other bridges were constructed as Hull grew beyond the confines of the Old Town. In 2011 we have 14 'bridges' – Sculcoates Bridge of 1875; Scott Street Bridge of 1902-03; North Bridge of 1931; Sutton Road Bridge of 1939; Drypool Bridge of 1959-61; Myton bridge of 1977-79; the Stoneferry twin bridges of 1989-91, and the Ennerdale twin bridges of 1996. Other railway or footbridges that span the river, are the River Hull Railway Bridge of 1885; Wilmington railway bridge of 1907; the Tidal Surge Barrier of 1980, and the footbridge at The Deep of 2009.

32 1929.363 (11.6 x 16 cm) right, and **33** 1929.371 (11.3 x 15.8 cm) below A 'more permanent bridge' across the Beverley & Barmston drain, was proposed to the Corporation in May 1875, and the new bridge opened in March 1878. These drawings of c.1880, show the new bridge, which linked Lockwood Street with Barmston Street. The larger drawing is from the north, and the smaller from the south. Built of wrought iron supplied by Bells, Lightfoot & Co of Newcastle, it was initially paved with wood from the Ligno Mineral Co, and the brickwork was by contractors Storry & Jagger.

Visible in both views is Glossop's Brewery, established as the Imperial Brewery by William & Robert Glossop in 1834. Ceasing brewing c.1903, the company was latterly known as William Glossop & Bulay (1933) Ltd – maltster's and malt flour manufacturer's – until closure c.1965. The brewery buildings, featuring windows engraved with sheaves of barley within the Lincoln Street frontage, survived into the 1970s. Now only an altered warehouse, at the corner of Northumberland Avenue and Westmoreland Street, survives. Fortunately the bridge was made a Grade Two Listed Building in 1994.

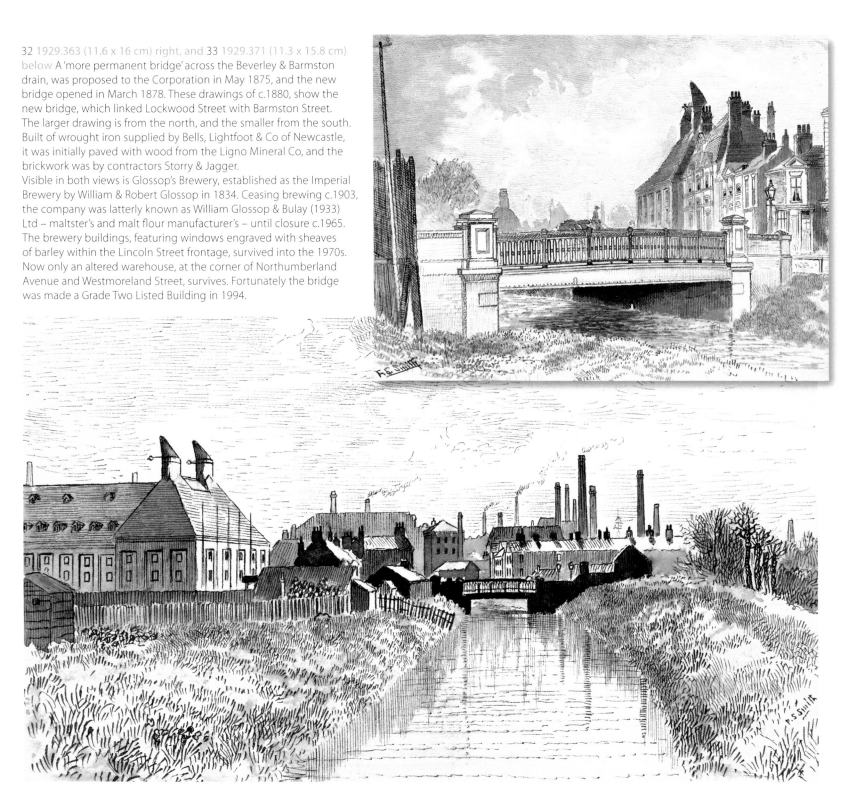

34 1929.370 (10.1 x 14.4 cm) Smith had only a short walk to make most of his drawings of the Sculcoates area, as his home address from c.1885 was Rose Street, at the north end of Waterloo Street. In this drawing of c.1885 he shows another of the agricultural drains that cut across this part of Hull – the Cottingham Drain – constructed in 1771. The bridge was probably located at this point to give access to a long-standing tannery, of which some buildings can be seen on the left of this drawing. Note how the bridge forms part of a wall, with a doorway giving access to the drain bank and a football pitch beyond. The pitch was laid out north of the tannery in the 1880s, directly in front of Finsbury Grove – a long terrace facing the drain, which can be glimpsed on the far right. The bridge led from the end of Providence Row – on the right, a small part of which survives. Dating from the late 18th Century, this is one of the oldest alignments off the Beverley Road, and was shown as 'sold' on Bower's plan of the area made in 1791, and mentioned by name in the trade directories from c.1814. A tannery was established here in the early 19th Century, and by 1823 another had been built, on the south side of the street. Both are shown on Baines' 1823 map, and Baines' 1823 directory names them as Benjamin Casson at no.13 Providence Row, and Edward West at no.12. West's tannery had been built upon by the 1880s, but Casson's old tannery, owned by the Holmes family from c.1870, survived in an extended form into the 1950s, when it too was built upon. The tall trees mark the grounds of Elmfield or Elm Tree House, built in the late 1840s for Benjamin Casson. A new street was laid out on the site of the house from 1889, extending north from the tannery, and over the site of the football pitch. It was named Holmes Street, in honour of the later tanners (see title page).

35 1929.172 (11.2 x 15.5 cm) An early morning scene in Cumberland Street around 1885, looking north towards Wincolmlee (then known as Church Street at this point). The tower of St Mary's church in Air Street, is just visible beyond the masts of ships, moored in the winding alignment of the River Hull. Cumberland Street was laid out from c.1822, creating a more direct route across Sculcoates – and an alternative to the long and winding Church Street. On the left, is the entrance to Westmoreland Street, laid out as part of the Kingston Estate in the 1870s. At the far end on the left, the tallest building visible was the Kingston Cotton Mills, established here in 1845 (see pages 34-35). As well as the Kingston Estate, there were many other references to the Kingston Cotton Mills in the area. Barmston Street was itself initially called Cotton Mill Street, and visible on the right (east) side of the street – marked by a flag-pole – is a pub called the Kingston Hotel, which is still open today over 150 years since it opened in 1848. Curiously, nearby Bromley Street was originally named Kingston Street – but was created many years before the cotton mills were built.

Just a few doors from the Kingston Hotel, was the Spinners Arms of c.1851, and other pubs in the street were the Prince of Wales of 1863, and Raywell Hotel of 1872, and directly opposite the south end of Cumberland Street – in Wincolmlee, was the Duke of Cumberland of c.1803. Other than the Kingston Hotel, only one or two other original buildings now survive in Cumberland Street.

36 1929.236 (11.3 x 15.7 cm) below, and **37** 1962.24.6 (14.2 x 19.9 cm) right North of Providence Row, was a strip of land belonging to John Wright Swann. Initially part of a huge area owned by the Egginton family, Swann acquired the strip as access to a larger area of land that he owned, between the Cottingham and Barmston drains. A long-established footpath ran across his land, to link with the older Egginton's Lane (see page 33) and was initially referred to by that name. This was developed as Fountain Road from the early 1870s, and named after Alderman John Fountain. Fountain Road is shown below, looking west towards the Beverley Road, in a drawing dating from c.1885. On the right is the Fountain Road Board School, of 1877. Closing in the 1960s, the school was demolished in 1981, when it had long been used as the Kingston Community Centre. It is shown right, in a drawing of c.1882 made from the junction of Waterloo Street, which bisected Fountain Road at this point, and was literally yards from Smith's family home.

38 1929.223 (10.2 x 14.3 cm) Smith made this c.1883 sketch further east, beyond the end of the 'new' Fountain Road, and the school and terraced housing in the previous sketch are clearly visible. Here, the old alignment that ran from the Beverley Road, was still no more than an agricultural track. Known colloquially as Egginton's Lane from c.1845, it had been in existence much earlier. The Egginton family were one of the largest of Hull's merchant dynasties, established in the whaling, oil, and seed-crushing trades during the early 18th Century. The family had land and an oil mill at the Church Street (Wincolmlee) end of the lane, which is shown on a plan of the area dated 1784, and they remained here until the 1860s. The mill is shown on pages 37 and 38. The fortified gate, with restricted entrances suggest that this was a halfpenny-hatch, where the Eggintons may have collected a toll from those who wished to cross their land.

In the late 1870s there was a growing demand for Egginton's Lane to be improved, and merged with the developing Fountain Road, creating a direct link from the Beverley Road to the River Hull, and industries in Church Street. This required new bridges across the Barmston, Cottingham, and Skidby drains, and the purchase of land through which the lane passed. It was eventually widened, by order of the Town Improvements Committee. Work began late in 1883, and continued into 1884, at a cost of around £8,000. Later improvements saw the original bridges replaced, one of which survives today and is dated 1889.

Sponsored by the East Yorkshire Local History Society (K.A. MacMahon Fund)

39 1929.372 (8.5 x 12.8 cm) Made at virtually the same time as the previous drawing, this is a view looking east along a footpath on the bank of the third drain in this area. The Beverley & Skidby Drain crossed Egginton's Lane, at a point behind Smith's position, then curved east towards the River Hull as depicted. On the left is the boundary fence shown on the left of the previous drawing – Smith's vantage point for this view, being outside the enclosed section of the lane. The small wooden footbridge led over the drain to the entrance of Cobden Place, another street that was laid out on a much older curving alignment. Early maps of this area often show a track marked as 'old footpath to Sculcoates Church', or similar. This led across land owned by Lister's Hospital, and was in part named as Lister Street (1852 Ordnance Survey) – a section later re-named Lockwood Street. From c.1846 the north end of the old path was developed with houses with large rear gardens, as the land opposite had been sold to the Kingston Cotton Mill Company, who developed a huge complex of cotton-milling buildings on the site from 1845. Cobden Place consisted initially of a terrace of around 16 houses, but the rear gardens were later built upon and surrounded by terraced housing, as the 'Kingston Estate' was developed around Northumberland Avenue and Westmoreland Avenue in the 1870s. Cobden Place, and the adjoining terraces – including some back-to-back housing, remained inhabited until the Compulsory Purchase Orders of the 1960s slowly eroded all housing from the area. Two of the three land-drains in this area were filled-in and culverted in the 1960s, and only the Beverley & Barmston Drain remains open in 2011, however some old railings can still be seen along the line of the Skidby Drain, in places along Fountain Road, alongside the boundary fences of industrial premises.

Sponsored by the East Yorkshire Local History Society (K.A. MacMahon Fund)

E J Smith
1889

40 1929.219 (13.2 x 19.2 cm) The huge complex of buildings that formed the Kingston Cotton Mill Company's premises, can be seen on the left of this 1889 drawing. Looking west into Egginton's Lane (now Fountain Road), Smith was stood at the entrance to the lane from Church Street (now Wincolmlee). The first stones of the buildings were laid in November 1845, according to the Hull Packet newspaper of the time, and the mills were still under construction in July 1846. The original buildings, with a main entrance in Cumberland Street, were 167 yards long, 28 yards wide and four storeys high along the Egginton's Lane elevation – shown in Smith's drawing. The four-storey buildings were split into three main sections, which held mule-spinning, roving-spinning and throstle-spinning machines, as well as winding and carding. The three sections were divided by two huge steam-engine rooms, standing four-storeys high. The chimney at the far end – the corner of Cobden Place – was 150 feet high,

and another at the south side of the site – just visible on the left of the drawing – was 225 feet high – reduced from its original 245 feet, following storm damage. The smaller buildings held amongst other things, a bundle room and baling shop, a mechanics shop, and a beam room and 'cop' warehouse. The mills were designed by James Lillie & Co, and the steam engines were built by the Soho Iron Works – both situated in Manchester.

The 1851 Census records reveal that only 16% of those working in cotton or flax manufacture in Hull, were actually Hull-born, with the majority coming from Lancashire, Cheshire and Ireland. The mill closed in 1894, and was used mostly as the Co-operative Wholesale Society's Preserve Works – known locally as the 'Jam Factory', until 1938. Many buildings had been demolished c.1898, but just as many remained, until the Blitz of the Second World War. One large block, 18 bays long and five bays wide, remained on the east side until c.1980.

41 1929.294 (13 x 19 cm) left, and 42 1929.280 (13 x 19 cm) below
Two drawings made in 1888, showing the Northumberland Avenue
Almshouses, constructed from 1886 for the Hull Municipal Charities
Trust, at a cost of around £15,000 (exclusive of the site). Built to the
designs of Brodrick & Lowther, work commenced late in 1886, under
contract to Mr Musgrave, and they opened in November 1887.
Intended as a replacement for at least nine of the older 'hospitals' within
the Old Town, that were being demolished at that time (see Chapter
3), the remote location of the new buildings was the subject of much
debate in the press at the time. The almshouses remain in use today.
Northumberland Avenue was laid out as one of the main roads of
the Kingston Estate, from 1877, along with Westmoreland Street and
Main Street, and was later extended to form an approach to the new
almshouses from Egginton's Lane (now Fountain Road).

43 1929.198 (129 x 92 cm) It is difficult to now imagine, the acres of housing that filled the area around the banks of the River Hull. The east of course, had its housing enclosed mostly within the Groves area, whilst that in Sculcoates spread west from the river, all the way to the Beverley Road. Some of that housing can be seen to the left of this c.1885 drawing, which depicts a view looking north along Church Street (now Wincolmlee), with the entrance to Oxford Street left of centre.

Just visible on the far left – almost hidden by the steps up to the ground floor of the houses facing the street – is what appears to be a cellar window. This was in fact the window of a living room, giving at least some sunlight, to a house that backed onto the Wincolmlee property. This was a cruel version of back-to-back housing, in which the developer sought to maximise profit on every square foot of land. The shallow two-storey houses that faced the street, had small sunken courts of equally shallow property, attached at the rear. By sinking the rear courts below street level however, another floor could be added, increasing the dwellings in the court to three-storeys. This short section of road between York Street and Oxford Street, had five such courts, each with two houses facing the street, and at least two facing the court. This was not an unusual style of housing in this area – indeed, the courts mentioned here, backed directly on to identical courts, that were in turn attached to the houses that faced Oxford Street.

These slum dwellings were recorded in a series of photographs made by the Health Department, which can be viewed in the Hull History Centre. Photographs of this area show that some of the dark tunnel entrances, which led via steps down into these courts, had keystones dated 1828; they were demolished c.1912.

At the time of Smith's drawing, the opposite side of the road – to the right of picture, was mostly taken up by oil seed-crushing mills. There were six between this point, and Sculcoates Bridge to the south, utilising the riverside location for supplies brought by river. On the right can be seen the Church Street Mill and yard, known as the Lion Mill at the time of Smith's drawing. This was one of the first oil mills in which hydraulic presses were used, in the 1820s. The mill was rebuilt several times, mostly as a result of fires, but survives in part, as the Lion Wharf and warehouses. This is an extremely rare survivor, in an area that has been systematically stripped of its many original industrial buildings.

In the distance, is the distinctive tower of the former Egginton's Oil Mill (see pages 33 and 38), at the corner of Fountain Road and Wincolmlee, a site still used for oils today as part of a Rix Petroleum storage depot.

44 1929.398 (11.1 x 15.5 cm) If one picture in this book illustrates the value of Smith's art – then it's probably this c.1885 view. Made from the original Wilmington railway bridge on Wincolmlee, it looks south towards Fountain Road. A short essay could be written about the aspects of Hull that Smith captured in this small drawing alone.

Church Street began at the north end of Wincolmlee, which originally ended at High Flags, and then followed the banks of the River Hull, to St Mary's Church (see page 39). Re-named as part of Wincolmlee from c.1890, the north end that is shown here, had surviving buildings that appear to date from the early 18th Century, and possibly earlier. These are the low buildings, with long dormer windows, on the far right, which had been adjoined or altered at some point,

with the two-storey building over an arch. This group of buildings may relate to the very first industrial development of the area, from the late 18th Century. It was then that tar & turpentine works, worsted and seed-crushing mills, colour-works and tanneries, were built all along this stretch, facing east across the river. Beyond the low buildings was the three-storey Ship's Hold Hotel – a pub that opened c.1822, closed around 1967, and was demolished in the late 1970s. Smith was no doubt making the drawing, as a record of the low buildings, as they were demolished before soon after this drawing was made.

The castellated tower is the former Egginton's oil mill, behind which can be seen the tallest of the Kingston Cotton Mill chimneys, and mill buildings. On the left, is a conical lime kiln, at Robert Freeman's sand and lime works, on the riverside.

45 1929.267 (10.8 x 15.3 cm) below, and **46** 1929.251 (15.7 x 23.5 cm) right Church Street (Wincolmlee) ended, as it does today, at the junction with Bankside and Air Street, in the old hamlet of Sculcoates. The larger of these two drawings, shows Bankside, looking south towards that junction c.1885. On the left, can be seen the unusual stepped gable-end of St Mary's Church School, built in 1852 in a vaguely Tudor style of architecture. This remained in use as a school until 1908, and the building remains, but has lost most of its decoration, and is now used as an industrial storage room. On the right of the larger drawing, was St Mary's Church, also shown in the smaller image – with Air Street running off to the left. Air Street, was the main street in the old hamlet of Sculcoates, and the eastern end of an old footpath between Cottingham and Sculcoates; little more than a track, that ran west from the river Hull, through the settlement built around the church of St. Mary. The dwarf wall and palisade was built in 1868, as Air Street was widened, replacing a much higher brick wall that had become unsafe, and that had fallen on several occasions.

47 1929.261 (11.2 x 15.7 cm) A rare view of the west end of St Mary's Church in Air Street, made from a vantage point looking east from Sculcoates Lane.
A church is mentioned in the ancient hamlet of Sculcoates, as early as the year 1232, although the building Smith drew dated from c.1759, with alterations made in 1827-30 and 1861-63, by which time it was the parish church of Sculcoates. The church ceased to be the parish church of Sculcoates in 1869, when the larger All Saints Church opened in Margaret Street, off the Beverley Road (see page 65). The churchyard of St Mary's was closed for burials in 1855, but a separate burial ground had been built in Sculcoates Lane many years earlier. Known as the Sculcoates Burial Ground, it was authorised in 1817, and was also known as the Sacristy – as it contained a central mortuary chapel. Although it was almost three acres in size, by 1866 this too had become 'overcrowded'. An extension of the burial ground was suggested, on former pleasure gardens adjoining the west side of the existing site, but this was never carried out. In 1868 an extension was instead consecrated, on 'glebe land' on the opposite side of Sculcoates Lane. In an interesting contrast to the peace of the cemetery, the former pleasure gardens – known as St Helena Gardens – had often been much more rowdy. In 1864, the proprietor of the gardens, Mr Isaac Denson – who regularly sold alcohol to visitors – was refused a spirit licence. Complaints were heard at the Brewster Sessions from local residents, and the minister and churchwardens of St Mary's, who noted that a spirit licence would 'increase the vice and immorality practised therein' and – 'that the gardens were and always had been improperly conducted, and were frequented by disorderly persons of both sexes'. Reports of illegal races, and gambling were also reported in the press, and later that year the garden's buildings and equipment were destroyed in a mysterious and 'disastrous' fire. The pleasure gardens – originally laid out c.1850 – remained until the 1890s, and obviously unaware of the previous misconduct, the long-closed cemetery is still often referred to, as the St Helena Gardens Cemetery.

3 The City Centre

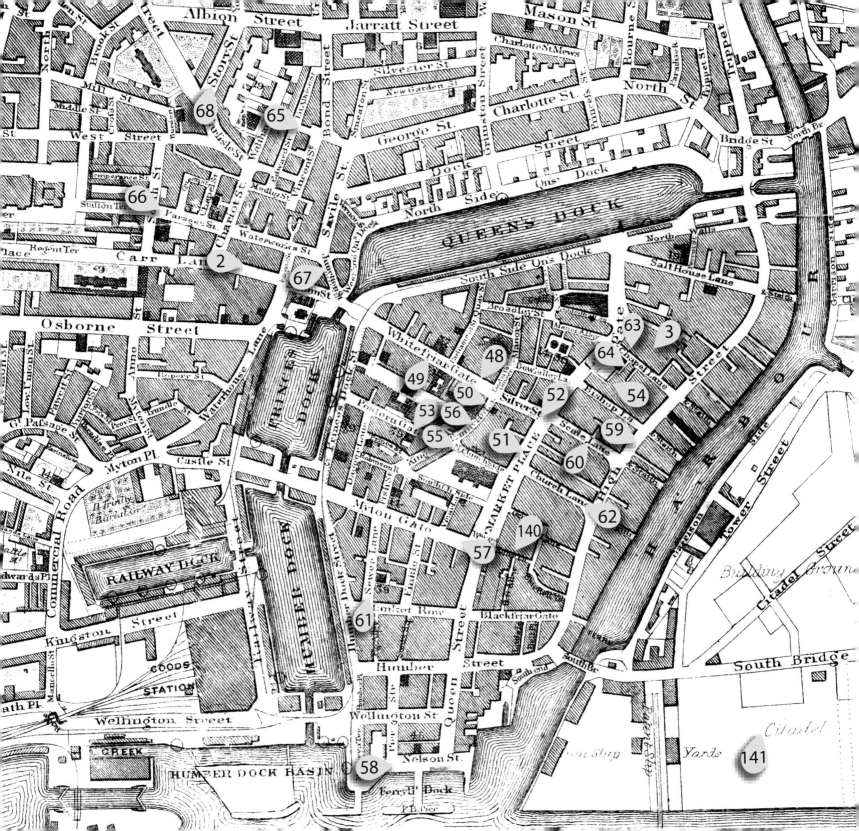

48 Chapter title page 1929.332 (13.3 x 19.2 cm) In 1829 the board of Trinity House voted to demolish and rebuild all of their property east of the former Neptune Inn (now Boots the Chemist), at the east end of Whitefriargate. The centrepiece of the new building, designed by Charles Mountain junior, was a bank – with four shops and houses on either side; the bank of Smiths & Thompson (established in 1784) re-located here from Wilberforce House in High Street. Shown in 1889, the site remained a bank until c.1906, and was latterly a branch of Woolworth's, and more recently Peacocks. Note the sculpture in the pediment, by Thomas Earle of Hull.

49 1929.333 (19 x 13.1 cm) left The Hull branch of the Bank of England opened on 2 January 1829, in a house in Salthouse Lane, later used as the Sailors Home. In 1856 it re-located to new stone-fronted premises, built on part of the site of the old Workhouse in Whitefriargate. This 1889 drawing shows the bank, designed by the bank's architect Philip Hardwick, which was situated on the north side of the street, near the entrance to Parliament Street. The bank closed on 28 February 1939, as the Bank of England decided that there was: 'no justification for maintaining the expensive organisation in Hull, or for incurring the considerable expenditure necessary if the Branch were to be modernised or rebuilt'. The building was demolished soon after closure, and the re-built site is now partly occupied by an HMV music store.

50 1929.336 (12.7 x 18.2 cm) right Joseph Pease & Son were Hull's first bankers, opening in January 1754 at premises in High Street, where they had long been merchants. This 1887 drawing shows their later premises, situated at the north end of Trinity House Lane, near the junction with Silver Street – known as Pease's 'Old' Bank, where they moved in 1838. This was rebuilt in 1897 to the designs of W.W. Gywther, and was latterly a branch of Barclays Bank. Converted to a pub in 2000, and named Lloyd's No.1, it is now known as the William Wilberforce.

51 1929.321 (19 x 13.5 cm) above The Post & Telegraph Office was situated at nos.5-7 Market Place, and was built in 1877 to the designs of J Williams. Its typically bold architecture, particularly the over-sized consoles supporting the door canopy, remain as powerful a statement today as in 1888, when Smith made this drawing. The building has long been a popular Italian restaurant, and is now known as 'The Old Custom House'.

52 1981.415.16 (24.3 x 16.6 cm) left This c.1882 scene, looking south along Market Place, may illustrate the equivalent of today's rush-hour. Cabs pass through the long early morning shadows, no doubt transporting merchants to their offices in High Street, and a cart on the right waits patiently outside the entrance to the Spread Eagle pub. In the foreground a single line of tram tracks curves out of Silver Street and into Market Place. These were horse-drawn trams, which operated on this route from the early 1870s.

53 1981.415.112 (13.2 x 18.5 cm) below Gregg's Hospital was situated on the south side of Posterngate, near to the junction of Trinity House Lane and King Street. The hospital was founded in 1414 by alderman John Gregg, and had 12 rooms – 'for 12 poor people'. A House of Commons report on the charities in Hull in 1833, noted that: 'the 12 poor women inhabiting this hospital are each paid two shillings a week, together with an annual supply of coal and turves' (dried turves or peat, were burnt for fuel). Smith shows the Posterngate elevation of the old hospital, with the premises of wine merchants Elam & Smith visible to the right. At the rear of the building was a large communal garden, which remains an open space in 2011, but is now a car parking area for private housing. Built on the site of the hospital in the 1980s, the development was named Andrew Marvell House. Pictured by Smith around 1887, Gregg's was one of several hospitals that were re-located to the more comfortable, and healthy environment, of the new Northumberland Avenue almshouses in that year. The 1881 Census – the last before the closure of the hospital – recorded 11 widows present at the old hospital, only three of who were Hull-born.

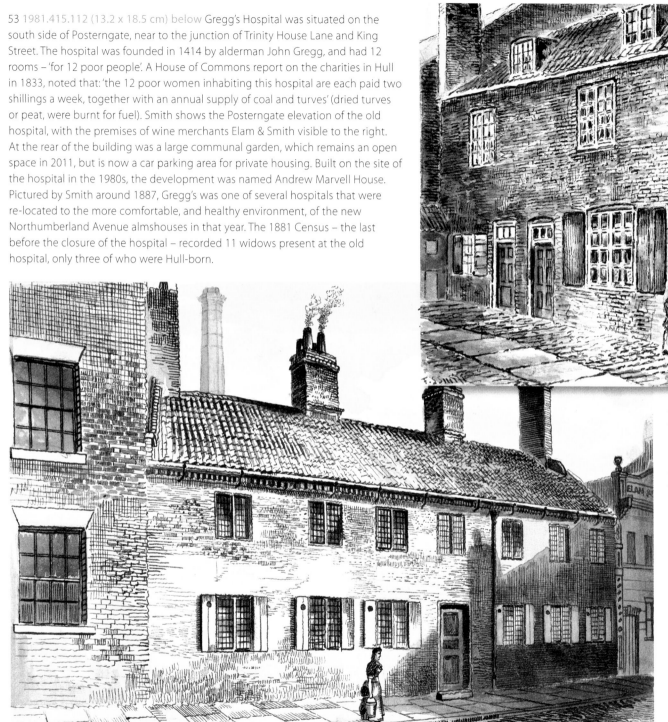

54 2006.7399 (14.3 x 15.2 cm) above This humble building was recorded by Smith, due to its importance as having been one of the first Post Offices in Hull. Situated within a small court, entered via a tunnel entrance between nos.25 and 26 Bishop Lane, it was in use as the Post Office as early as 1814. By 1834 the Post Office had moved to premises in Land of Green Ginger (now a hairdressers), to more accessible premises in Whitefriargate in 1843, and to the premises shown on the previous page in 1877. The court in Bishop Lane was given the name Old Post Office Entry.

55 1929.227 (11 x 13 cm) King Street originally ran from Trinity House Lane to Fish Street, with terraced property on both sides, and an alley giving access to Holy Trinity churchyard. A Hull Packet report in May 1876 commented: 'we may soon now have good-riddance of bad rubbish, for surely the unsightly consumptive-looking houses, with bill-posting decorations and broken windows, have offended the eyes of both residents and visitors long enough. We have all been wondering how it was [that] such a miserable forsaken pile should have remained on end so long, blocking one of the most splendid views of our newly restored parish church'.

The east side of King Street was demolished in 1876, leaving just nos.1 and 2 standing, opposite the Kingston Hotel – visible on the left. Merchant Thomas Keyworth joined wine & spirits merchant Harriet Freshney, at no.17 King Street c.1855, to form Freshney & Keyworth. From c.1870 simply Keyworth & Co were listed, at nos.1 and 2 King Street, remaining there until it too was demolished c.1886. As Keyworth, Walker & Co, they remained at premises on the opposite side of street until 1897, now also demolished. Smith was recording nos.1 and King Street c.1885, as a record of the property just prior to its demolition.

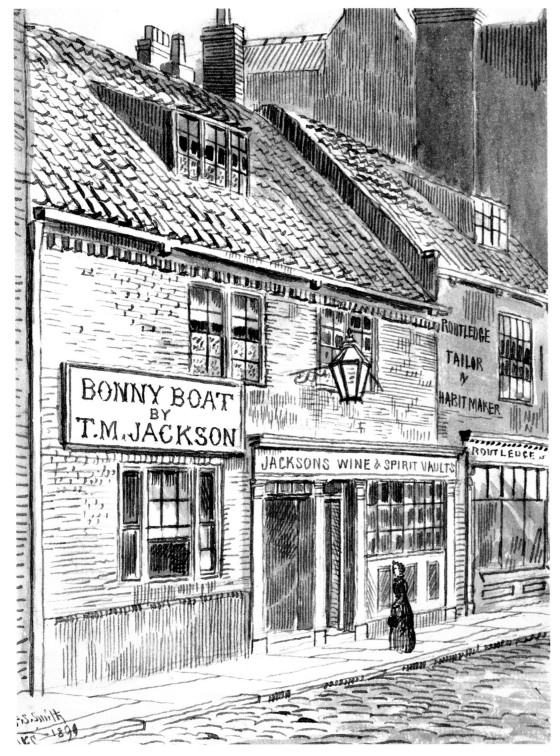

56 1981.415.31 (16 x 11.8 cm) Smith's sketch of the Bonny Boat pub in Trinity House Lane is dated December 1890, and captured a valuable record of the original building just weeks before it was demolished .

Trinity House Lane was first known as part of 'Old Beverley Street', but is recorded in property deeds as 'Sewer-side' in 1591, and by 1644 as 'Trinitie House Lane'. The 'Guild or Fraternity of Masters and Pilots, Seamen of the Trinity House of Kingston upon Hull' – known simply as Trinity House since 1581 – established property on the south side of Whitefriargate in 1461. Trinity House acquired all of the land up to the line of 'Sewer-side', and hence it took the name Trinity House Lane sometime between 1591 and 1644.

Hollar's 1640 plan of Hull, shows a building on the site of the Bonny Boat pub, and it is possible that this is the building that Smith shows in this sketch.

The Bonny Boat is recorded as a pub in trade directories from 1791, and takes its name from an event in 1613, when Captain Andrew Barker, an 'elder brother' of the Trinity House, was at sea in a whaling ship off Greenland. Here he discovered an exhausted local, afloat in a canoe or kayak. Captain Barker took him on board, but he died three days later; his small boat, belongings and clothing were returned to Hull, and are still on display within Trinity House.

At the time of Smith's drawing, the last landlord of the pub had been Thomas Mathew Jackson, who was there from 1880 until c.1890. The old pub was demolished in 1891, and rebuilt as we see it today at the start of a phase of town improvements, which resulted in the construction of the Covered Market Hall in 1902.

As was often the case during these improvements, a number of important buildings were lost; some were in need of removal, such as Trinity Buildings – a court of 16 cramped and insanitary dwellings directly behind the pub – and Shipham & Co's brass foundry – adjoining the north side of the court-housing, which belched noxious fumes all across the town. However, another of Hull's old almshouses, known as Watson's Hospital was also lost. Dating from 1690, the hospital faced North Church side, adjoining the south side of the court-housing of Trinity Buildings.

57 1929.108 (15.4 x 11.6 cm) Drawn by Smith when he was just 24 years old, this view of Mytongate in 1883, is unrecognizable today. Even the name was erased, when the street was demolished in the late 1970s, to create the Castle Street dual-carriageway, which so effectively isolates all of those buildings south of its four busy lanes of traffic. Only two original buildings survive from the original street – the former Hull Corporation Telephone Department of 1904, and the second building on the right in Smith's view – marked by a large lamp outside. The obligatory large gas-lamp was often a sign that this was a hotel or pub, the light enticing or guiding punters to its welcoming doors.

This was once known as the Britannia Hotel, no.83 Mytongate, which started out as a small beer-house, established by Thomas Marshall in 1830. The adjoining property (no.82) was acquired by Marshall c.1844, and the whole re-opened as the 'Union Coffee House and Queen's Hotel', also licensed as a Dram Shop in the 1850s. From c.1874 it was more famously known as the wine & spirits stores of Evelyn Cooke, who re-fronted the buildings in the elaborate, Italianate, 'Gin-House' style of the period. It was then that it became known, as what we would call a 'pub'. The Britannia was shut-down in 1913, and was taken over by Joseph Dalton & Co, provision merchants. £677 was claimed in compensation for the closure, but only £425 was paid.

The building was left in a precarious and isolated position, following the demolition of all that surrounded it in the late 1970s, and was latterly used by Burnett & Co (as Burnett House). The name Evelyn Cooke could still be seen on the gable end, until recently, when it was renovated to a high standard. It remains unused and mostly hidden from view by hoardings. Other pubs marked by large-lamps in smith's view, were the Black Swan on the immediate left, and beyond the Britannia Hotel on the right – the Victoria Vaults, near the corner of Vicar Lane. Visible on a projecting sign is the name Spikins; this was the shop of house-furnisher, George Spikins.

58 1929.25 (11.3 x 15.6 cm) Smith made this sketch of Nelson Street c.1885, and the long shadows in the foreground, suggest his visit was at the end of the day. Earlier in the day, this view would have been filled with passengers using the ferry, visitors to the pier, carriers' carts ferrying goods to and from the market boats in the Horse Wash, and men visiting the many pubs. A dominant element in the scene, is the cast iron urinal on the left. These ornate, dark green structures, standing eight feet high, first appeared on the streets of Hull in the 1850s. Although a few brick-built urinals existed slightly earlier, the first mention of public toilets in the Hull press, appears to have been in October 1853, when a report noted: 'the making of a number of public urinals was referred to the Committee of Works to carry into effect'. By January 1854 'two iron urinals similar to those in Glasgow' had been ordered. This new desire to cater for the lack of facilities, was no doubt instigated by a stinging report from a local doctor (MacMillan), regarding the general state of health in Hull. Following his report the Council quickly appointed its own Sanitary Committee, with Dr Ayres as its chairman. The first two cast-iron public urinals in Hull were erected in 1854 at King Street, alongside Keyworth's building (see page 46), and here in Nelson Street. The costs incurred were: 'wages £111-17-9, cart hire £62, materials £61-18-4, tradesmen £9-17-0, and the two urinals £25-9-11.' The cast iron urinal was replaced with the present brick building, in 1926, at a cost of just over £2,500.

59 1929.287 (22.7 x 13.3 cm) An early 1880s drawing, showing the arched entry between nos.46 and 47 High Street – on the east side, almost opposite the end of Scale Lane. The decorated finish, mostly in brick, suggests that the building on the left dated from the 17th Century; the courtyard of the former Coach & Horses Hotel that stood in the Market Place, had identical features dating from c.1660. The site of the buildings and entry, now stands vacant at the north side of Scale Lane Staithe, having been demolished in the 1930s.

60 1929.345 (19 x 13.5 cm) A drawing dated 1889, showing no.30 Scale Lane. The Hull Packet was first produced from here in 1787, printed and published by George Prince. The York artist William Etty served an apprenticeship here from 1798, with later printers of the Packet, Thomas Lee and Robert Peck. The building survives, minus its top floor, as Ruskin Chambers – having been substantially altered, and re-named in the early 1920s. On the right is a tunnel entrance, which also survives, that once gave access to the houses in Broad Entry, Narrow Entry and Stewart's Yard.

61 1929.40 (9.1 x 12.9 cm) This street was part of an alignment known as Beverley Street – predating the construction of the town's defences c.1320 – and winding north through the town, much the same as High Street. Known as Ogger Lane and Sawyer Lane in the 17th Century, the name Sewer Lane came into use in the 18th Century. The watercourse that inspired the name 'sewer', and caused the curving alignment, was revealed during archaeological excavations in 1974. From the late 18th Century it had been home to clock-makers, tailors, cabinet-makers and hairdressers, but at the time of this c.1885 drawing, looking north from the Blanket Row end of the street, the traders in Sewer Lane had changed considerably. The trade directory of that year lists 10 butchers, a tripe dresser, a cattle salesman, a hide broker, and two pubs in the street – by then at the heart of an area known for its many slaughter-houses, which remained until the 1950s.

On the right is Crowle's Hospital, founded in 1661 by alderman George Crowle, and possibly the first building in the street. Built in the Artisan Mannerist style, in 1833 there were 14 inhabitants in the 12 rooms, who were paid two shillings and six-pence per week, plus an 'allowance of coal and turves'. In 1890 Historian Edmund Wrigglesworth noted: 'the walls are three feet in thickness', and – 'a room formerly used as a chapel is lined with oak panels and has a massive oak door'. Above the door were two stone tablets, one of which read (in Latin): 'give freely while you've time, and use a generous hand'. Crowle's Hospital transferred to the new almshouses in Northumberland Avenue in 1887, and this historic old building was sold in 1902, and demolished soon after.

Next to the hospital was the Tap & Barrel pub, also known as the Golden Barrel, Railway House, and Scarborough Arms. Opening c.1803, the pub closed c.1895.

Sponsored by the Hull Maritime Society

62 1981.415.7 (18 x 13.7 cm) The 1891 Census lists Joseph Rudkin, as a 59 years old chimney sweep, with his wife Betsy at their shop and home at no.17 Church Lane; also present – their two sons, and three daughters. The family moved to no.12 Church Lane c.1892, as shown in Smith's drawing, which is almost certainly of that date. Showing clearly the number and name of the premises, and the proprietor at the door, Smith may have been commissioned by Rudkin to adapt a version of his drawing for display in the shop; something Smith is known to have done as a part of his work. Joseph remained in charge until 1900, but the 1901 Census notes a change in circumstances, as Betsy was by then the head, but listed as a widow. Her two sons were still at home, and by 1905 William Rudkin is listed as a sweep at no.12. In 1910 the business expanded, when William and John were listed as chimney sweeps from no.21 Craven Street, leaving Levi Rudkin and his four sons, and two daughters at no.12 Church Lane. Levi was probably the bother of William and John, and he continued to be listed in the trade directories, as a sweep based in Church Lane until the early 1920s. Several of the Rudkin brothers remained in the chimney sweeping trade until the 1950s. Smith's drawing shows the street looking east towards High Street, which can be seen in the distance. Also in the street c.1892 was the Market Tavern, Winn's Temperance Hotel, and the extensive premises of wine & spirits importer John Coulthart. On the north side of the street was the Juno Tavern – opposite Rudkin's – and the adjacent premises of Ginner, Morton & Goddard – 'colonial produce merchants', and various other small shops. Chapel Lane suffered badly during the Second World War, and the 1949 Ordnance Survey plan shows it 50% demolished. The remaining buildings were swept away from c.1973, in preparation for the King William House development, which included the adjoining multi-storey car park, and a Habitat shop (now more familiar as an Argos store).

63 1981.415.8 (13.5 x 19 cm) right Alderman John
Harrison left funds in his will for a hospital, that was built
on this site in 1550, and gave funds for the ten rooms
'for the habitation of poor women'. Known as Harrison's
Hospital, it was situated on the south side of Chapel
Lane, directly behind St Mary's church, and was rebuilt in 1723 as it appears in this drawing. Church Alley,
which can be seen on the right of Smith's 1888 drawing,
remains to this day, whereas the former almshouses were
sold by the charity trustees in 1898, and demolished
in the early 20th Century, following the removal of
the facility to the new almshouses in Northumberland
Avenue.

Hull Lighting now occupy the site of the almshouses,
as well as the three-story building shown to the left of
the drawing; known as Standidge Buildings, this was
constructed c.1886 as a multi-purpose complex, and in
1888 it was occupied by book-binders, bag merchants,
and importers of various goods. Other than St Mary's,
this is now the only original building left in Chapel Lane.

64 1929.278 (13.5 x 19 cm) left
At least 13 almshouses existed within
the old town, many dating from the
16th and 17th Centuries. Following the
amalgamation of nine almshouses to the
Northumberland Avenue site in 1887, all
of the former almshouse buildings were
sold and later demolished. There are
now no surviving examples of these old
almshouses left in Hull.

Fox's Hospital, was built in the rear yard
of Harrison's Hospital in 1795, by a widow
– Mrs Mary Fox. This provided an extra
four rooms, and is shown here in another
drawing made in 1888.

The 1891 Census reveals that both
Harrison's and Fox's former hospital
buildings, were rented privately, following
closure in 1887. Listed as Harrison's
'Buildings' and Fox's Almshouse, they were
uninhabited, or had been demolished by
the time of the next census in 1901.

65 1929.132 (11.6 x 15.5 cm) The feature that gives a clear date for this drawing, is the scaffolding in the centre distance, as construction of the original Savings Bank, at the corner of George Street and what was then Smeaton Street, began in May 1883 (now Lloyds TSB). To understand this view, use the map on page 42, as most of the alignments have changed drastically. Smith was looking east, towards George Street in the far distance, and the cart was stood in the entrance to Bond Street, which ran west, and then curved sharply off to the left of this drawing (due north). Continuing west from that point, in the foreground of the drawing, was Davis Street. On the far right, at nos.5 and 7 Davis Street, was butcher and provisions dealer William Rufford, and further on – with the morning sun streaming through – the entrance to Vincent Street.

On the opposite corner of Vincent Street, was the Tally-Ho pub – no.26 Bond Street – adjoining more shops on the south side of the Bond Street entrance. Most of the buildings in the foreground on the right, were demolished in 1901, for the construction of Jameson Street. The Tally-Ho survived, and was re-built in 1901, and remained open until 1957. The pub, and remaining buildings centre-left, were all demolished in 1957, when the awkward entrance to Bond Street was cleared, and the street was widened to create the present dual-carriageway.

66 1929.154 (11.4 x 15.4 cm) Paragon Street was begun in 1802, but not fully built upon until the 1860s. On the far left of this c.1885 drawing, the clear gas-lamp marks branch no.11 of the Hull People's Public House Co – a temperance society – in a building later known as the White House Hotel, but currently empty. Beyond that, another gas lamp and flagpole marks the St Leger pub, at the corner of Little Queen Street. Further lamps mark another four pubs along this north side of Paragon Street, before the junction with Waterworks Street and Chariot Street; the Pavilion Hotel, Railway Inn, Brunswick Tavern and the Neptune Hotel.

The impractically large 'New Amphitheatre' opened in 1846, and was described in The Builder magazine in 1861 as: 'a huge magnified doll's house – both common and tasteless'. Reduced in size, and re-named several times (Royal Amphitheatre, Theatre Royal, Queen's Theatre), the theatre had a long and successful life as the Tivoli Music Hall from 1912, closing as the much-loved 'Tivoli' in 1954.
On the right of the picture is the Imperial Hotel, constructed in 1878 on land made available by the partial demolition of the Theatre Royal. The Imperial Hotel was redeveloped as the Hull Centre Hotel c.1967, and is now The Portland Hotel.

67 1962.24.17 (32 x 21 cm) below In 1867 a London architect Christopher George Wray won the first prize of £100, in a competition to design new Dock Offices for Hull. Replacing Hull's second Dock Offices in Dock Office Row, which had been in existence since 1820, the new buildings were erected in Junction Street on a site formerly occupied by shops and houses. Excavations for the foundations began in January 1868, and by March 1869 the as-yet unbuilt cellars of the new building were being advertised to-let as: 'suitable for Wine or Ale & Porter Merchants'. The cellars were still vacant in November 1870, when the advertisement was repeated. Built in a new 'fire-proof' style, the offices opened on Thursday 5 October 1871, and cost around £90,000 to build. Closing in 1968, the offices have been used as a museum since 1975, and fittingly, will house the 2011 F. S. Smith exhibition.

68 1929.414 (14.2 x 16.2 cm) above Built as a private house in the 1780s, this building on the west side of Story Street, was in use as a 'ladies day and boarding school' by 1867, under the supervision of the Misses Jemima and Miriam Roberts.

Amongst the residents present at the school on the evening of the 1871 Census were: two housemaids, a cook, the head school mistress, a French mistress, a music teacher, and nine students aged between 11 and 16 years. The school was listed as nos. 20½ and 21 Story Street in the census, and the boarders came from as far afield as Grimsby in Lincolnshire, and Doncaster in West Yorkshire.

From 1873 the buildings were used as the Hospital for Poor Sick Children – later named the Victoria Hospital for Poor Sick Children – until 1891, when a new larger hospital was built in Park Street. The arched panel over the main door in the drawing, shows wording relating to the hospital, and this would suggest a date for the drawing of c.1891, when the hospital was removed.

From that point, it was home to a variety of institutions until c.1910, when it became a short-lived theatre known as the Shakespeare Hall. At that time it was also simultaneously the meeting place of – amongst others – the Hull Dickens Fellowship, Hull Dramatic Society, Hull Geological Society, Hull Scientific & Field Naturalist Club, Hull Junior Naturalist Society, and naturally – the Shakespeare Society. The theatre ceased to be listed at the time of the First World War, but the building – although much-altered – still survives. The left, or south, side of the building is presently unoccupied, and the right (north) has long been the home of Greensmith's stationers – established in 1945.

4 Beverley Road & the Avenues

69 Chapter title page 1929.155 (11.8 x 14.6 cm) Horse-drawn trams operated on the Beverley Road and Spring Bank from 1875. In this c.1883 drawing, a set of tram lines curve out of Prospect Street and west along Spring Bank, where the entrance to Spring Street can just be seen on the left. Another set of lines head north (right) into the Beverley Road, passing Blundell's Corner and the old shops.

70 1929.194 (11.3 x 17.7 cm) above An early Smith drawing, dated 1883, this early morning view depicts the original narrow entrance to the Beverley Road. Smith was looking north, from the end of Worsley Street, which was demolished in the late 1950s. On the left is a small pub, that was established c.1800 as the Windmill Inn, changing its name c.1861, when the census of that year recorded William Lait and his wife, at the Park Hotel no.9 'Beverley Street'. The pub closed c.1901, when several buildings here were demolished for an extension to Blundell's paint works. The entrance to the Hull Daily Mail car park now marks the spot. On the right is a long terrace of 13 houses, that were gradually being converted to shops at the time of the drawing. This was Lansdowne Terrace, built c.1845, and bisected by Norfolk Street as seen on the right. The section far-right, was demolished c.1958, but the section beyond Norfolk Street remains in 2011.

71 1929.207 (9.6 x 12.2 cm) The alignment of Norfolk Street is shown un-named, and with no property, bisecting Lansdowne Terrace on Stephenson's 1842 plan of Hull. It was first mentioned by name in the local press from 1844, and by the census of 1851 most of the street was inhabited. Entering Norfolk Street from the Beverley Road, the first building on the right is now a pub called The Lamp. Four branch police stations were built in Hull during the 1870s, and this was the first – proposed in June 1876, but not opened until July 1878. The first men in alternate charge at Norfolk Street, were sergeant Shipinson, and sergeant Parrott (who lived at the station). Provision was made in the design of the station for a

fire engine, and this was the first headquarters of the Hull Volunteer Fire Brigade in the late 1880s; note the two arched entrances (now closed) at the west (right) side, in Smith's c.1888 drawing. The Corporation loaned the volunteers a manual fire engine, hose and other equipment, but the service soon moved to larger premises in Hall Street, and the force was disbanded due to financial difficulties in 1891. Norfolk Street station was disused before the Second World War, but was used as the location of an air-raid siren. From c.1950, the former station was used as a club, variously known as the New Waltham Club (1950), Oliver's (1982-85), Jailhouse (1990), Blue Lamp Music Club (1992), and from c.1996 as The Lamp.

72 1929.415 (11.9 x 18.7 cm) A rough sketch by Smith, possibly made as a guide for a later detailed study, showing a section of the Beverley Road that we now forget was once private housing. On the far left is the entrance to Trafalgar Street – laid out in 1852 at the south end of York Parade. York Parade dated mostly from c.1820, and 10 houses are shown in this section on the 1852 survey plan, most of which can be seen in this drawing. Smith may have been recording the scene prior to the construction of the Beverley Road Baptist Church, built at the corner of Trafalgar Street and the Beverley Road in 1905-06. The church, which still survives in 2011, required the demolition of the first three houses on the left, and

the two adjoining houses are now the only ones that survive in York Parade. Since November 2010, the double-fronted no.53 Beverley Road (with bow-windows) and the adjoining no.55 (with curved two-storey bow front), have been home to the Hull Alcohol Recovery Treatment centre (HART).
At the far end of York Parade can be seen the Beverley Road Wesleyan Chapel, opened in January 1862, which closed in 1941 following minor Blitz damage, and was used as a printing works until a fire left the building in ruins in 1953. The site was cleared, but part of the front wall – and a school building of 1865 survive, now a Masonic Hall. The front elevation of the church can be seen on page 63.

73 1929.346 (13.4 x 19.1 cm) Several large detached houses were built along the Beverley Road in the middle of the 19th Century, and some high-quality terraced housing such as Kingston Terrace. Architect Henry F. Lockwood advertised his new terrace in the summer of 1840, as: 'a uniform line of 12 good houses, varying in frontage from 24 feet to 30 feet, with gardens to both north and south. Bounded on the west by the Beverley Road, on the north by the property of Henry Blundell esquire, on the east by open fields, and on the south by Kingston College. As the improvement of the neighbourhood is more the object of the proprietors than profit, the land will be sold at a very moderate price.'

Only four of the proposed 12 houses were ever built, all in 1841; a large house with garden facing the Beverley Road, and three adjoining terraced houses facing south across an even larger garden.

Shown here in 1889, Kingston Terrace was demolished for the Brunswick Avenue Board School begun in that year, and the Brunswick Arcade shops (of 1890), which remain, facing the Beverley Road.

74 1929.129 (13.4 x 19 cm) Just north of Kingston Terrace, was this much older house, built c.1828 facing the Beverley Road for the paint manufacturer Henry Blundell. Later known as Brunswick House and Hanover House, it was affected by the development of the 'New Brunswick Estate', begun in 1873.

J T Robinson, an architect based in London, though noted as 'late of Hull', proposed a boulevard, 45 feet in width running east from the Beverley Road to the Cottingham Drain. The new road would have two streets running at right angles across the boulevard, and 'Mr Blundell's house' was to be raised a storey and divided to form two family houses. The main road was named Brunswick Boulevard (later Avenue), and the side-streets were Clifton Street and Blundell Street. It's unlikely that Blundell's house was ever altered, as the last occupant was Henry Gleadow (of Hull Brewery) until c.1886; Smith shows it in 1889, shortly before demolition. A terrace of single-storey shops (Gleadow's Arcade) was built along the old frontage in 1894, and stables at the rear survived until 1982. Now, just a stone gate pillar remains, adjoining a wall marking the original property line.

75 1929.190 (13.2 x 19 cm) right, and 76 1929.229 (9.8 x 13.1 cm)
below A view of a fully developed Brunswick Avenue, looking west in
1888 (right), and an earlier view from c.1885 (below) – where the rear
of Brunswick House can be seen on the right of the picture.
A dispute arose in 1875, when two parties both wished to build pub
in Brunswick Avenue, on sites just 60 yards apart. The dispute went on
until 1880, but both applications ultimately failed, and the avenue only
ever had an off-licence. However, it did have a 'working-mens reading
room', which can be seen below left, at the corner of Blundell Street.

77 1981.415.69 (16 x 23 cm) left The Northern Branch Library opened in June 1895, which is very likely to be the date of this drawing. Built on a vacant plot of land on the east side of the Beverley Road, just beyond Fountain Road, it originally sat alongside the Sculcoates Union Workhouse. The ornate Late Gothic architectural style of the library, by architect H A Cheers of Twickenham, is unusual in Hull, and totally different from the Western Library, which opened in the same year. The first librarian was Mr Ernest Callard, and by 1910 the library held 12,000 books – more than any of the branch libraries at that time.

The importance of the library as part of Hull's architectural heritage, was recognized in 1994, when it was awarded Grade Two Listed Building status. In 2005 it was one of several libraries that were closed – its future uncertain for a short time. Fortunately an agreement was reached with nearby Endeavour High School in 2006, and the old building – now suitably restored – forms part of the school campus.

78 1981.415.70 (12.9 x 18 cm) right
A hotch-potch of individual, and semi-detached houses, once formed a section of the Beverley Road known as North Parade. Stretching from Providence Row in the south, to Fountain Road at its north end, the line of North Parade is shown on plans of the early 1800s. Seen here in 1896, is Burnham house (right) – built c.1840, and latterly home to Mrs Theresa Dawson, who was listed in the 1891 Census as a 78 years old widow. Next door, were bricklayer Benjamin Nicholson, and joiner William Preston. Burnham House was demolished in 1897, for the construction of Jubb's drapery store, which remains today. On the far left is a beer-house that was rebuilt in 1898, as the Swann Inn (now closed).
The house of the joiner and bricklayer, was demolished for the construction of the National Cinema in 1914, which remains in part as a Blitz-damaged ruin.

79 1929.256 (11 x 15.3 cm) below, and **80** 1929.260 (9.1 x 12.8 cm) right

Margaret Street is shown by name on the 1852 Ordnance Survey plan of Hull, but it was not until c.1861 that any houses were occupied. A church was first proposed for the street in 1861, and All Saints Street – directly opposite the church – was laid-out by 1863. The new church was intended to front the Beverley Road, but land was donated within Margaret Street free of charge, by Reverend John Jarratt. Building began in 1866, to the designs of G E Street of London, and the Church of All Saints opened in August 1869, immediately becoming the new parish church of Sculcoates. It is shown (right) from the east c.1882, and below from the west in 1883. The larger 1883 drawing, shows the tower that was added in that year. Closing in 1974, the church was quickly demolished; housing known as Cavendish Square was built on the site in 1983.

81 1929.308 (11.3 x 15.8 cm) At the end of Margaret Street is Park Road, which is shown as Park Street on an 1848 plan, and on the 1852 Ordnance Survey plan. Its name suggests that it may have been named as it leads to the south entrance into Pearson Park, however the park was only begun in 1860 (see page 74). This 1883 drawing, shows a view looking north along the road, from the corner of Margaret Street, with the former parish school of All Saints Sculcoates on the right. This was built in 1872, and taken over by the School Board in 1876, when it was altered and enlarged to the designs of William Botterill, to accommodate the increased number of pupils. The school was demolished in the early 1980s. Beyond the school is the entrance to Terry Street, and further along, the entrance to Cave Street. In between the two entrances, a railway crossing can just be seen. This was the York & North Midland Railway Cos. Victoria Dock Branch Line, heading north to Stepney Station; the crossing gate pillars are just visible at each side of the road. At the far end, beyond the original park gates, is the rear of one of the large Pearson Park houses, known as Kingston Villa. Much of the housing in the foreground has now gone, but most survives beyond Terry Street.

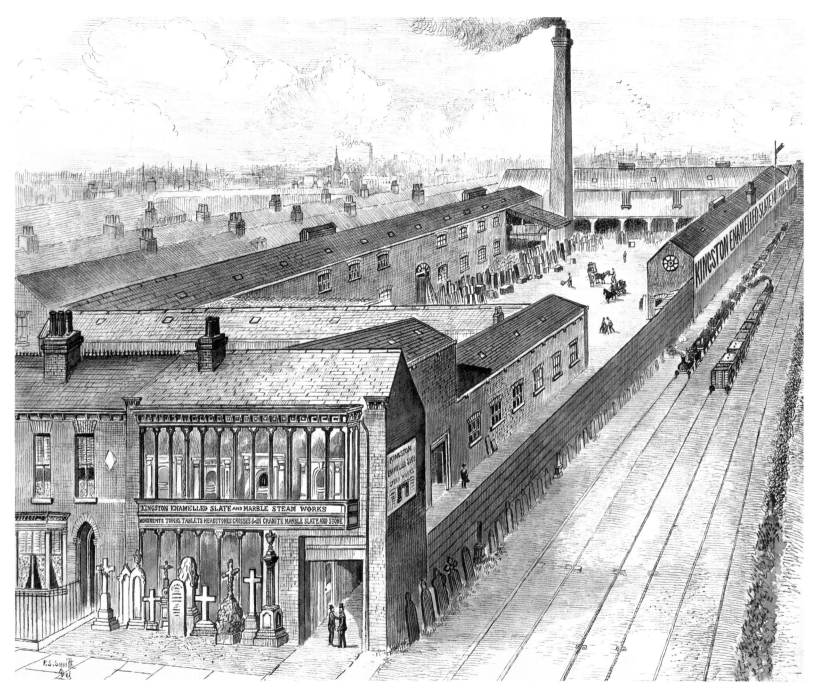

82 1981.415.78 (22.8 x 6.7 cm) At the north-east side of the level-crossing on Park Road, was the premises of the Henry Hare's 'Kingston Enamelled Slate & Marble Steam Works'. Established here in 1878, the company supplied marble and enamelled slate fire surrounds, as well as baths, cisterns, urinals, and lavatories.

Another line of business was the supply of 'tombs, tablets, headstones and crosses', also displayed at their 'Monumental Depot' on Spring Bank. Shown here c.1890, in a drawing that Smith would have been hired to create, the steam works closed c.1913. The site was then used as a Motor Garage, lasting until the 1970s.

83 1929.233 (11.4 x 15.5 cm) 'Leicester Place', appears on the 1852 Ordnance Survey plan, with three large mansion houses on its west side, which can be glimpsed in the distance, on the right of this 1883 drawing; this initial development marked by a line of trees in the centre of the road. The first of the houses was Leicester House or Lodge, occupied by William Summers and his family, including two sons who were both in the seed-crushing business. Next-door were Leicester Cottages, occupied by the Misses Anne and Sarah Ayre, and an adjoining property where solicitor John Saxelbye was resident. Leicester Street was developed as an extension of Leicester Place; one of three streets developed between Wellington Lane and Margaret Street from c.1867.

By the time of the 1871 Census, these were still the only houses in the street, and it was not until the late 1870s, that the other houses shown in Smith's drawing were built. The property shown on the left, appears as one terrace, but was divided by name into Ada's Avenue, and Arthur's Grove. These houses faced an open area – marked by the wooden fence on the right – until the Hull Grammar School re-located to a purpose-built school there in 1892. The Grammar School remained until 1953, and this is now used as the Pearson Primary School. Only the mature trees on the right remain from Smith's view, as the housing in Leicester Street was demolished in the early 1980s, including the last of the three large mansion houses – now lost beneath the extended school playing fields.

84 1929.191 (8.6 x 12.7 cm) In the foreground on the right of this drawing, is the entrance to Pendrill Street, which was laid-out in 1878. On the left is the entrance to Terry Street – laid out on the line of a pre-existing agricultural path, and named in honour of a former mayor Avison Terry, following his death in 1866. Beyond Terry Street is a set of gates – one topped with a gas-lamp – marking the level-crossing over the York & North Midland Railway Cos. Victoria Dock Branch Line, laid in 1852. The level-crossing also relates to the Stepney Railway Station, just out of view off the left of the drawing, also built in 1852. Designed by William Botterill, who came to Hull as the railway company's architect, this is now Hull's last surviving suburban passenger station.

In what seems like a rare but minor misjudgment, Smith has aligned the level-crossing gates on the left, slightly out of line with those on the right. Both appear awkward in relation to the signal box pictured, constructed in the late 1860s. Continuing north, beyond the signal box, can be seen the side wall of the Station Inn, a pub that was established here c.1870 by the wonderfully named Marmaduke Windross, and still popular today, although re-fronted in the early 20th Century. Other than the signal box and the chapel on the right, almost all of the buildings shown in Smith's drawing of c.1885 survive. The railway line closed to passenger traffic in October 1964, and to goods traffic in October 1968, but a large part of its route survives as a cycle track.

85 1929.189 (10 cm x 14.2 cm) Looking south towards the city – in the opposite direction to the last drawing, here Smith illustrates the heart of an area that became known as Stepney. It is likely that the small group of buildings that developed here – a hamlet quite independent of the town of Hull – was due to its location at a point where several long-established routes converged. Stepney Lane (left) and Park Lane (right), originally formed a route from the dairy fields of Newland Tofts and Chanter Ings – east to the 'Bull Fields' between the Beverley Road and the River Hull; the old lane giving access to fresh grazing for the dairy herds on the meadowland there. Crossing this old route was the Hull to Beverley road, which probably developed as the hamlet of Sculcoates was established nearby, during the 12th Century.

The name Stepney, and Stepney Lane, may have been taken from Stepney

Lodge, the home of James Rogerson, which is mentioned in a 1796 newspaper article. Situated on the north side of the lane, it was demolished c.1912 for the construction of Fenchurch Street, and the site is now the location of the car park of the Fenchurch Street Centre.

On the right, at the entrance to Park Lane, was a double-fronted office building – the premises of bottling engineer Thomas Hill at the time of this c.1884 drawing. Just visible beyond that is the Rose Tavern, in its original form, before being rebuilt for Moors' & Robson's in 1912, with its distinctive tower. Across the road was the Stepney Methodist New Connexion Chapel, built in 1869, which closed in 1966, and was demolished in the 1970s, along with the adjacent terrace of shops. Latterly this site was built upon by a branch of Kwik Save (c.1982), and more recently has been converted to a thriving multi-cultural supermarket.

86 1929.234 (9 x 12.5 cm) It is very likely that the Bull Inn at Stepney, took its name from the previously mentioned Bull Fields, that were once situated to its east, leading to the banks of the River Hull. Work had just begun on the terraced housing in Stepney Lane, at the time of Smith's drawing, but the vast majority was built in the early 20th Century. Many of the side-streets and terraces were given names that complimented Stepney, such as Fleet Street and Fenchurch Street. The pub had probably been in existence many years, before it was first listed in the trade directories in 1810, when Robert Jackson was noted as the victualler. However, no buildings are shown in the area we now know as Stepney, on Tuke's map of Yorkshire in 1786. First recorded as the Spotted Bull, this was soon simplified to 'The Bull', which it has remained for over 200 years.

The Bull Inn was used as a staging post for coaches, to and from Beverley and York, and thrived on the influx of workers required by the industries that grew around Sculcoates and Stepney during the 19th Century. Evidence of this industry can be seen over the roof of the Bull, with the tall chimney of J.R. Mayfield's huge Stepney Paper Mill, and the smaller mills visible beyond the end of Stepney Lane. Shown on the sign-board of the pub, is the landlord's name, this was James Nutt and he was victualler from c.1879 until c.1884, which suggests that the drawing was made c.1883. In 1902-03, and by then a Moors' & Robson's pub, the Bull was rebuilt as we see it today. Redesigned by architects Freeman, Son & Gaskell, and with the work costing £1,650, the quality of the rebuilt pub led to its award of Grade Two Listed Building status in 1994.

87 1929.291 (13.2 x 18.8 cm) At the opposite corner of Stepney Lane to the Bull Inn, was a plot of undeveloped land, shown empty in the previous drawing of c.1883. This was soon to be built upon, with the construction of the Beverley Road Board School, and as the date-stone within the dutch-gable of the school shows, it was completed in 1886. Smith's drawing was made in 1888.

The idea of a school on this site was by no means a popular one, and when the school was first proposed in 1884, several petitions were gathered by local residents. As the land had already been purchased, the Corporation proceeded with their plans, and by October 1885 tenders were being invited for the construction of the new school. At a meeting of the Hull School Board in January 1886, it was agreed that the tender of G S Skinner be accepted, whose quote

was for £7,425. In addition to Mr Skinner's costs, a further £250 for heating, £307 for furniture and fittings, £200 for a portion of the surveyor's and clerk of work's salaries, and £200 for extras, were all added – making a total of £8,382 to be requested as a loan from the Education Department.

Beverley Road was very similar in design to Crowle Street School (see page 19), as the architect was once again Mr Botterill. The initial accommodation was for 320 boys, 320 girls, and 255 infants – later increased to 1,211 places by the addition of a new junior block in 1908. Average attendance was 1,043 in 1911, which had dropped to 681 by 1938. The boys were removed in 1953, to the newly created Wilberforce High, leaving senior girls, mixed junior, and infants departments. Still in use in 2011, the school is now known as the Stepney Primary School.

88 1929.218 (11.3 x 15.7 cm) below, and **89** 1981.415.71 (25.2 x 22.7 cm) right The northern half of the vacant plot at the top of Stepney Lane (shown on page 71), can just be glimpsed to the right of this 1883 drawing. This was the site of the Beverley Road Baths, constructed in 1904. The larger image shows the scene looking north, away from Stepney, towards the junction of Queen's Road and Sculcoates Lane. On the far left are some of the Beverley Road's finest surviving houses – built in the 1870s – although most have long been converted to multiple occupation and/or business premises. The tallest building – with the distinctive turret – is on the corner of Pearson Avenue, and was known as Claremont Villa. Built c.1878, the first occupant was William C Croft, latterly a partner in H & W Croft: 'coal fitters and proprietors of the Darley Main Collieries'. Croft's business partner Henry Croft, lived opposite at Dorchester House, and both remained here until c.1887. Following Croft's departure, Claremont was home to a Gas Superintendent, and latterly a Wholesale Iron Monger, until conversion to flats in the late 1930s. The still striking house, now forms part of a nursing home known as Rose Villa (nos.269-271 Beverley Road), which includes the adjoining house. The smaller Claremont drawing is of c.1920.

90 1929.187 (10.1 x 13.9 cm) left Pearson Park was the 21st provincial park to be built in England; Derby's Arboretum, which opened in September 1840, was the first. Such was the popularity of Hull's first public park, that it was not unusual for 6,000 visitors to come to the park on an average Sunday during the 1860s.

The park opened in August 1860, and a public holiday was declared on the opening day. The list of attractions for the two-day fete (Monday and Tuesday) that accompanied the planting of the first tree, included three military bands, a firework display, and artistes such as 'Madame Geneave Saque', who 'made her terrific ascent on the fiery rope 60 feet in height, surrounded by prodigious jets of flame and coloured fires'. Admission on the first day was by ticket, at a cost of two shillings. Shown left c.1883, is one of the original refreshment pavilions, built c.1881, located on the site now occupied by the adventure playground; note that the flag is marked 'Park Pavilion', and in the background is Prince's Avenue.

91 1929.210 (10.4 x 14.2 cm) right
The great rise in popularity of the British Brass Band, occurred during the middle of the 19th Century, and the increasing number of public parks provided a natural framework for their recitals. The band-stand shown here c.1883, was erected in 1881, located on a prominent piece of land on the west side of the lake, opposite the refreshment rooms shown above. Designed by the Borough Engineer, with removable shutters, the band stand cost around £105 to build.
It was re-located to the centre of a specially created formal garden area c.1907, which survives alongside the present 'Victorian Conservatory'.
The band stand was probably removed during 'modernisation' of the park, which begun in 1950, when many other 'outdated' features were also removed.

92 1929.204 (14 x 10.2 cm) **below** The building shown in this c.1883 drawing was built early in 1862, by James Jackson at a cost of £272, and designed by architect Richard George Smith. A Park Keeper was employed in 1862 at a salary of 52 guineas per-annum – 'house rent and taxes free' – and this was his lodge. The first park keeper was Ralph Burton, who was recorded here in the 1871 Census, aged 56 years, with his wife and grand-daughter. An 1872 directory notes that he also ran refreshment rooms at the park. The lodge is now a Grade Two Listed Building.

93 1929.353 (11.8 x 15.8 cm) **top-left**, and **94** 1929.197 (11.3 x 15.5 cm) **bottom-left** Built in 1863, and costing £185 this second lodge was built at the west entrance to the park. Also designed by R G Smith, it was home to head gardener Edward Amos Peak. The 1871 Census recorded him here aged 38 years, with his wife, five sons and a daughter; by 1879 he was being paid 27 shillings a week. The lodge was altered to the designs of architects Smith & Brodrick c.1890, as shown in the lower drawing. Also visible are the ornate west gates, built by Thompson & Stather of Hull.

95 1929.221 (11.5 x 15.6 cm) left Prince's Avenue looking north, around 1883. On the right, was a plot of land at the end of Hinderwell Street, that remained empty until c.1898, when the present terrace was built, and in the centre, one of the Avenues' six fountains, that was removed in 1926.

96 1929.230 (11.5 x 15.7 cm) below Work began on the Avenues' – or Westbourne Park Estate – in 1874, and Salisbury Street was one of the first to be built. On the right of this 1883 drawing, are some of the Queen Anne style houses, designed by George Gilbert Scott junior, and built c.1878 for his cousin John Cooper. Cooper was a Hull solicitor, and one of the first occupants of the Gilbert Scott houses. Barcombe House and Tower house, visible at the end of the street, were built c.1879. Tower House, on the right, was demolished c.1915, but Barcombe House survives in 2011 as an NHS centre. From the 1960s, Scott's houses were gradually converted to flats.

97 1929.216 (11.3 x 15.6 cm) right More of the Gilbert Scott houses can be seen in this drawing, also of c.1883, showing the junction of Salisbury Street and Westbourne Avenue. Looking north-west, it shows the undeveloped nature of the estate at that time, with very few houses and very young trees.

98 1929.193 (11.2 x 15.6 cm) below Another 1883 view of Westbourne Avenue, looking south-west towards the fountain that was built in 1874. The 1881 Census recorded 24 properties in Westbourne Avenue (including 11 empty houses that were probably waiting to be let), and nine properties in Salisbury Street. Tower House and Barcombe House were listed within Salisbury Street, as was Tofts Farm, a property that pre-dated the development of the Avenues', near the Victoria Avenue junction. The other houses listed in Salisbury Street – those by George Gilbert Scott junior – were still mostly unoccupied at the time of the 1881 Census.

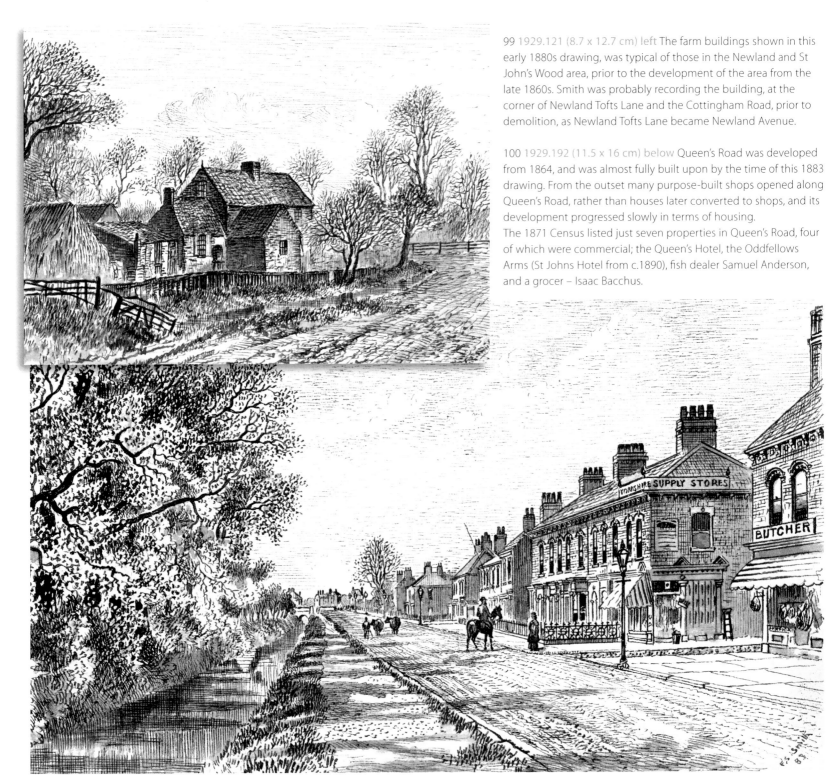

99 1929.121 (8.7 x 12.7 cm) left The farm buildings shown in this early 1880s drawing, was typical of those in the Newland and St John's Wood area, prior to the development of the area from the late 1860s. Smith was probably recording the building, at the corner of Newland Tofts Lane and the Cottingham Road, prior to demolition, as Newland Tofts Lane became Newland Avenue.

100 1929.192 (11.5 x 16 cm) below Queen's Road was developed from 1864, and was almost fully built upon by the time of this 1883 drawing. From the outset many purpose-built shops opened along Queen's Road, rather than houses later converted to shops, and its development progressed slowly in terms of housing.
The 1871 Census listed just seven properties in Queen's Road, four of which were commercial; the Queen's Hotel, the Oddfellows Arms (St Johns Hotel from c.1890), fish dealer Samuel Anderson, and a grocer – Isaac Bacchus.

101 1929.325 (11.5 x 15.8 cm) below The Beverley Road in 1883, with the entrance to Queen's Road on the far left. On the right is the entrance to Sculcoates Lane, and in the distance the high-level railway bridge of the Hull & Barnsley Railway Co – erected here just a year or so earlier. On the left is the Queen's Road Wesleyan Chapel of 1878, which closed in 1967, and is now the site of Queen's House flats.

102 1929.123 (15.5 x 11.3 cm) right Beyond the high-level railway line, the Beverley Road was still relatively undeveloped in the early 1880s. Smith's c.1883 drawing, shows the section approaching the Cottingham Road and Clough Road crossroads, as little more than a dirt track at that time. On the left is a house that now houses a take-away Pizza outlet, and just to the right of centre – the old Haworth Arms, in its original position further east. Just visible over the roof of the Haworth Arms, is the ornate tower of Endsleigh House, built for brewer William Glossop c.1876, and later more well-known as Endsleigh Convent from c.1901.

103 1929.242 (13.3 x 19.1 cm) above This 1889 drawing shows the junction of the Beverley Road, with the entrance to the Cottingham Road on the left, and Clough Road on the right. The cart is travelling south along the Beverley Road, into Hull. The open view of St John's Church was lost when the crossroads was redeveloped in 1926, and a William Jackson's shop was built on the corner, obscuring the view.
George Houlton & Son built the Jackson's shop, and at the same time demolished the old Haworth Arms – visible on the opposite corner, which had become a hindrance to modern traffic levels. They also built the present Haworth Arms during the demolition, thus maintaining its licence by never closing.

104 1929.200 (15.5 cm x 11.2 cm) right This earlier view, drawn in 1883, shows the same junction as above, but from the east. Looking west out of Clough Road, and across the Beverley Road into the Cottingham Road, it illustrates the rural nature of this area at that time. The wall on the left marks the boundary of Newland Grove, one of Newland's finest houses, and now the site of the Grove House residential care home. Clough Road, as its name suggests, led from the Newland Clough (a small gate or sluice), through which the Newland Beck drained into the River Hull. It also served as part of the road that linked the old stone ferry over the river, via the Cottingham Road, to the village of Cottingham. A fence alongside the Newland Beck, can just be seen at the edge of the Cottingham Road, in the centre-left of the picture.

1889

5 West Hull

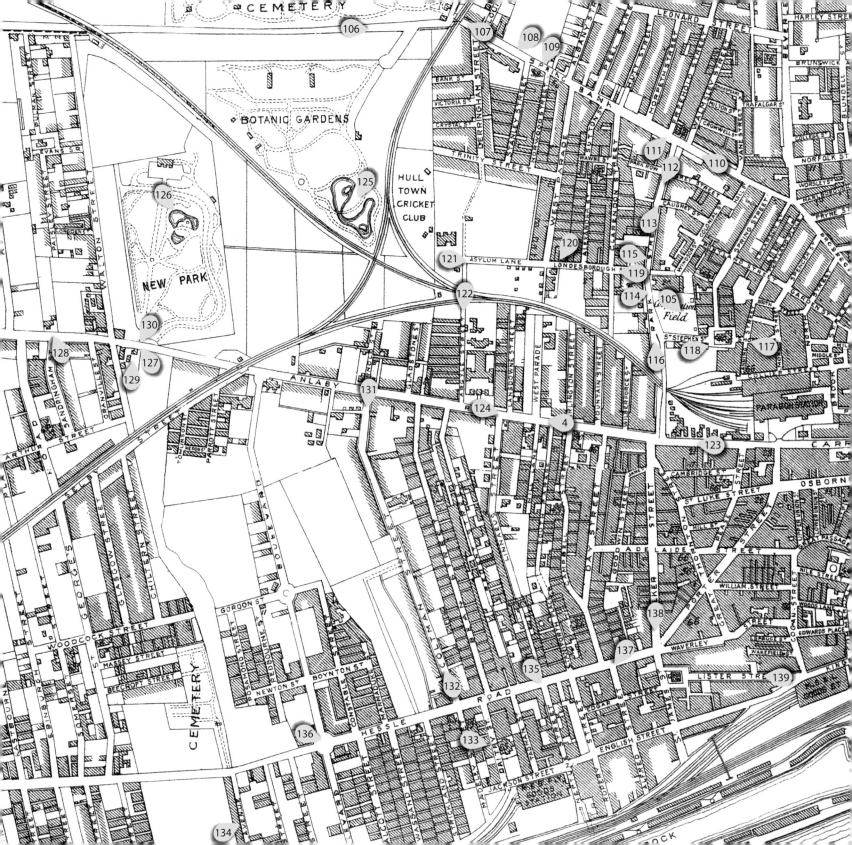

105 Chapter title page 1929.239 (15.7 x 19 cm) A large field on the east side of Park Street (then known as Elm Tree Avenue) was donated by the town authorities c.1838, for use during the town's spring fairs and for gatherings and meetings. Initially it was used for livestock fairs, and sales of horses, foals and cattle were recorded in the papers by 1848. The field became known as the 'Corporation Fair Field', and was home to the present October Hull Fair from 1865 until 1888. The field was later supplemented with covered areas and permanent surfacing, but ceased to be used from 1958, and the site is now lost beneath the St Stephen's development. Smith shows the field in 1889, looking east from Park Street towards St Stephen's church (see page 91).

106 1929.157 (11.2 x 15.7 cm) The lane shown in this 1883 drawing is overgrown with grass in the roadway, suggesting very light traffic at that time. The modern scene is quite different, as this is now the busy Spring Bank West – historically known as Springhead Road and Spring Bank. As the development of Spring Bank spread beyond the junction with Prince's Avenue in the 1880s, this semi-rural area was also built upon, with housing for Hull's increasing suburban population. Water had been brought to the town of Hull, via the Spring Ditch, from the wells at Springhead since at least 1538. Paths or tracks, created from the spoil when the ditch was first excavated, were gradually formed along the banks of the ditch. Situated on both sides of the 14 feet wide ditch, these tracks were well-used by locals, but accidents and drownings were a regular occurrence. Though the ditch had been covered further east by 1831, it remained open from Prince's Avenue to Springhead until the 1880s. The town's water-house – built in 1616 – was removed from Waterworks Street to a site on the right of this view in 1830. The short-lived Stoneferry Waterworks took over from Spring Bank in 1845, taking its water from the River Hull. For several reasons – not least the cholera outbreak that ravaged the town in 1849, Stoneferry was closed and Spring Bank re-opened in 1858. The existing Springhead Waterworks (latterly a museum) were constructed from 1862, and the waterworks at Spring Bank corner became disused; the site was later purchased by the railway company.

The fence on the right leads towards a signal box, situated at the level-crossing shown on page 84, and beyond that can be seen the twin towers of the Ebenezer Primitive Methodist Chapel on Spring Bank. On the left, the wooden fence and mature trees mark the boundary of the Hull General Cemetery.

107 1929.209 (11.2 x 15.6 cm) This 1883 drawing, shows the level-crossing over the railway lines of the York & North Midland Railway Cos. Victoria Dock Branch Line (laid in 1852), and the entrance to the Hull General Cemetery, which opened in 1847. On the left is Spring Bank West, and to the right Prince's Avenue. On the far right was the newly built Osborne Villa, home of sculptor and monumental mason William Day Keyworth junior, who was 39 years old in 1883. His father, William Day Keyworth senior, was then aged 65 and living at no.54 Savile Street above their offices; the 1881 Census notes that William Day Keyworth & Son then employed 14 apprentices. Both father and son studied in London, at Sir Francis Chantrey's studio. William senior returned to Hull in 1834, and was soon in business as a sculptor and modeller. Initially at no.28 Junction Dock Street, by 1842 he was resident in Baker Street, and from c.1852 was listed as an 'architect and sculptor' at the Savile Street address. By 1882 Keyworth & Son had the yard at 244 Spring Bank, offices in Savile Street, a studio in Paragon Street, and premises in London where William junior was latterly based. William senior had four brothers, including Joseph Milburn Keyworth (born 1825), who was listed as a sculptor's apprentice in the 1841 Census, and went on to become a stone mason. Brother Charles, died in infancy, and another brother, Edward John Keyworth (born 1833), also became a stone mason. Brother George (born 1819) became a Whitesmith, but his son Joseph (born 1850) became a stone mason, and was listed at another yard at 224 Spring Bank from c.1881 until the early 1920s. William senior retired to Hornsea, where he lived until his death in 1897, and by 1900 only William's yard – shown in Smith's drawing – was listed in the directories; sadly, William Day Keyworth junior committed suicide in 1902.

108 1981.415.80 (12 x 16.7 cm) left The Hull Mariners Church Sailors Orphan Society, had intended to build an orphanage since at least 1860, initially planned for Castle Street. Following a substantial donation from ex Hull shipping company owner John Torr, their hopes were fulfilled and plans revised. Built on an acre of land on the south side of Spring Bank, which was donated by Trinity House, the foundation stone of the orphanage was laid by Mr Torr on 30 March 1865, and it was officially opened in October 1866.

Mr Torr nominated the London-based architect Thomas Henry Wyatt, who being in his late fifties in 1865, in turn appointed the Hull architect William Kerby to supervise the build on his behalf. The building contract was given to Benjamin Musgrave, for a sum of £3,200, and extensions by Smith & Brodrick were added in 1876-81. Seen here c.1883, the orphanage transferred to Hesslewood House in Hessle in 1920. Known colloquially as Government Buildings, many of the rooms here were used as offices, and remained in use until demolition in 1989-91.

109 1929.252 (18.5 x 26 cm) right St Jude's Church mission services, had been held in a room at the Spring Bank orphanage since c.1867, until a temporary church was built on a site east of the orphanage, in the summer of 1869. Funds for a more permanent church were continually being raised, and in September 1872 the foundation stone of this church was laid by Charles Henry Wilson MP.

The church was finally opened in May 1874, following delays due to unstable foundations. Designed by Edward Simpson of Bradford, the church was constructed by Hockney & Liggins of Great Union Street, at a total cost of around £3,750.

St Jude's was demolished c.1974, but the church hall of 1925 survives as part of a frozen food store, which also utilises the site of the former church as its customer car park.

Sponsored by ADR Sound Sense

110 1929.158 (11.3 x 15.5 cm) This 1883 drawing shows Spring Bank looking west. Horse-drawn tram lines can just be seen diverting slightly – beyond the entrance to Freehold Street on the right – avoiding a line of the trees in the centre of the road. These were Lime Trees, planted on the line of the old Spring Ditch when it was filled-in in 1831, following the establishment of the new waterworks at the end of Spring Bank in 1830 (see page 83).

Spring Bank was not a road at that time, but a footpath along the raised bank of the old ditch. From the moment the ditch was filled-in, regular requests were made to the Corporation to convert the widened footpath to a more accessible 'boulevard' for use as a healthy walking area for the locals. It was not until 1846 that the Corporation thought the expense worthwhile, and the footpath was gravelled. At that time it was suggested the Lime Trees be taken out, and more

suitable trees be set at either side of the widened thoroughfare. New trees were gradually placed along the developing road, but many of the Lime trees remained until the 1920s. Set awkwardly along the centre of the widened Spring Bank roadway, they had become a problem for trams and the increasing number of motor cars, and were removed.

On the left is the original narrow entrance to Park Street, beyond which can be seen the frontage and roof of the Spring Bank Presbyterian Church of 1875. This Gothic church, designed by Smith & Brodrick, closed in 1931 and was used as a warehouse until demolition in 1966. More recently the site has been occupied by Kwik-Fit Tyres, which opened in January 1989. On the right is another of Spring Bank's five original churches, the Jubilee Primitive Methodist Chapel, which is described on page 87.

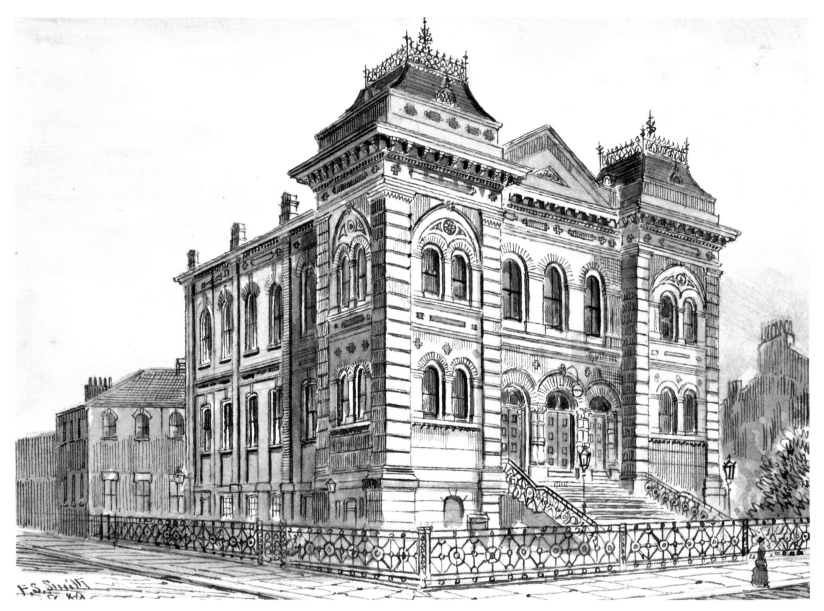

111 1981.415.81 (12 x 17 cm) On the right of the previous drawing – the north side of Spring Bank – can be seen this building; the Jubilee Primitive Methodist Chapel, erected in the corner of a field owned by paint manufacturer Henry Blundell. A huge Italianate chapel, of red and white brick with stone dressings, it was designed by Joseph Wright and is very similar to one of his other chapels – the Bright Street Chapel on the Holderness Road, which was already under construction as the foundation stone of this chapel was laid in February 1863 (see page 16). The builder of this church was Robert Bailey of Goodwin Street, Tadman & Wallis of Anlaby Road were the stone-masons, Wilde & Son of Queen's Dock Side were the slaters, and the joinery was by Stamp's of Barton upon Humber; the whole works costing £6,100. The chapel was demolished in 1958 and replaced by the present more modest building, which is now known as St Stephen's Church. On the left of the chapel is Freehold Street, begun from the north end in the late 1850s, but only extended south alongside the chapel in the late 1870s. The basement floor of the chapel held a school room, an infant school room, and seven class rooms, and on the left of this 1889 drawing is the former Sunday School. Built in 1881, this more easily maintained building has out-lived the original chapel, and remains in regular use as St Stephen's Church Hall.

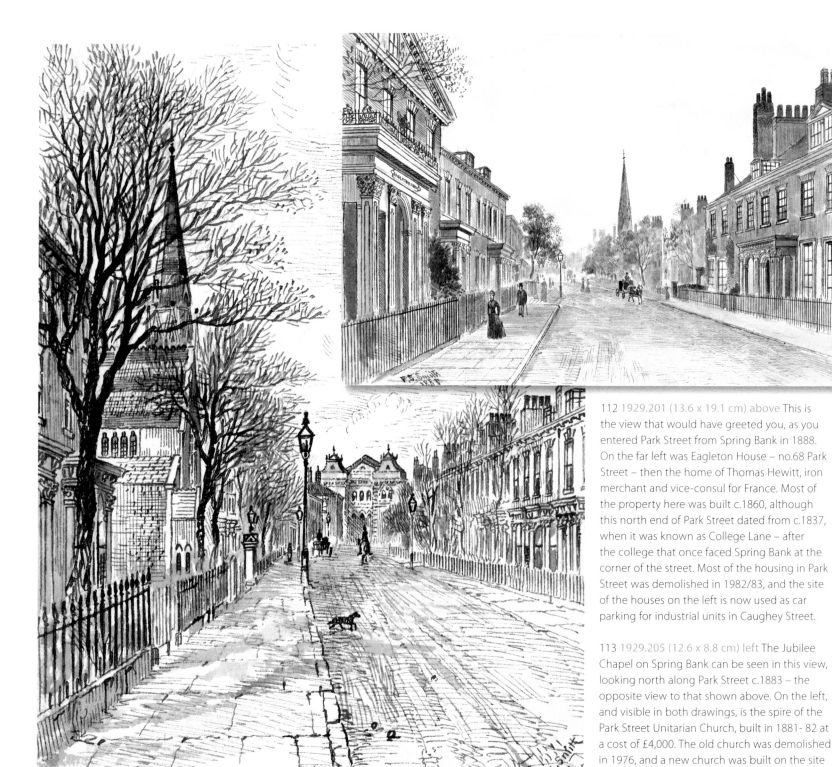

112 1929.201 (13.6 x 19.1 cm) above This is the view that would have greeted you, as you entered Park Street from Spring Bank in 1888. On the far left was Eagleton House – no.68 Park Street – then the home of Thomas Hewitt, iron merchant and vice-consul for France. Most of the property here was built c.1860, although this north end of Park Street dated from c.1837, when it was known as College Lane – after the college that once faced Spring Bank at the corner of the street. Most of the housing in Park Street was demolished in 1982/83, and the site of the houses on the left is now used as car parking for industrial units in Caughey Street.

113 1929.205 (12.6 x 8.8 cm) left The Jubilee Chapel on Spring Bank can be seen in this view, looking north along Park Street c.1883 – the opposite view to that shown above. On the left, and visible in both drawings, is the spire of the Park Street Unitarian Church, built in 1881- 82 at a cost of £4,000. The old church was demolished in 1976, and a new church was built on the site in 1977, which remains in use today.

114 1929.356 (12.7 x 18.1 cm) At the north west corner of the Corporation Fair Field, was a building constructed to house the 'Working Men's Art, Industrial and General Exhibition', held from June to December 1870. The Corporation provided the land free of charge and the buildings were built with funds from the Working Men's Exhibition committee. Smaller exhibitions had been held around Hull, and locally at a girls school room in Spring Street since 1865, instigated by members of an adult night-class begun in 1851. Following the apparently poor management of the 1870 exhibition, and the lack of public support (partly due to severe criticism of the exhibition in the local press, regarding the lack of 'local' exhibits) the organisers were left with large debts. To clear the debts the building was sold for £700 in February 1871, to the 4th East Yorkshire Artillery Volunteers (who had previously met at the Corn Exchange in High Street) for use as a drill hall. The Corporation leased the land to the volunteers, who improved the wood and felt structure, by concreting the walls and slating the roof. The barracks, although greatly reduced in size, remained in use until demolition c.1958.

115 1981.415.67 (13.5 x 19 cm) In 1865 draper Edwin Davis acquired an almshouse known as Lister's Hospital, at the rear of his store in Market Place. Following some legal wrangling, in 1867-68 the shrewd Mr Davis agreed to build new accommodation for the 12 inhabitants of the old hospital – at his own cost – in return for the buildings and land in South Church Side. The new buildings were constructed opposite Mr Davis' home in Park Street, on a field that he already owned. Situated to the north of the Park Street Barracks, almost at the corner of Colonial Street, the new buildings were far superior to those they replaced, which dated from 1642, and had become very dilapidated. Designed by R G Smith, the new and larger buildings provided each inmate with two rooms, instead of the previous one.
Mr Davis did well from the sale, as not only were the former almshouses retained as showrooms for his business (until demolition in 1870), but he also sold-off architectural salvage from the demolition; he later donated £950 to the trustees. In 1887 (probably the date of this drawing), the inhabitants moved to a new municipal almshouse site in Fountain Road, and in 1889 the building was adapted as a girls charity school, remaining as the Cogan School until closure in 1950.

116 1929.184 (9.5 x 13.1 cm) At the foot of the Park Street road bridge over the railway lines, stood one of Hull's many ornamental fountains. Shown here in a drawing of 1885 looking north, the fountain appeared on Pettingell's Birds Eye View of Hull made c.1880, and it may have been in place some time by then. An article in the Hull Packet in August 1880, reported on a Council meeting where it was suggested that: 'considering the convenience of the public, [we] recommend the removal of the drinking fountain in Park Street to some more appropriate site; the council be requested to move the fountain to a site opposite the Hull & East Riding College'. However, the fountain remained for some time,

as in June 1884 a complaint was recorded in the same newspaper: 'whilst in the vicinity of Park Street Bridge I would call attention to the state of the drinking fountain stationed there. Let the weather be as wet or dry as possible, there is always to be found round the well a large lake of water, and generally a group of dirty youngsters paddling in it, and playing with the filthy liquor, greatly to the annoyance of passers-by. Surely something can be done to improve this quarter of the town. I'm sure it's much in need of it.' Following further complaints about the poor condition of the fountain, it was finally removed in 1885, causing Smith to make the fountain the focus of his drawing, as it was about to be removed.

117 1929.253 (13 x 9 cm) right, and **118** 1929.237 (12.7 x 18.5 cm) below In April 1842 architect Henry F Lockwood invited tenders in the press, for the: 'several works required in the erection of St Stephen's Church', and the first stone was laid on 3 June 1842. Work was delayed in November 1843, when 20 feet of the 90 feet spire was blown down in severe gales, and the official opening finally took place on 11 April 1844. The contractors were Myers & Wilson of Carr Lane and Queen Street. Shown on the right, is the east end as viewed from Short Street c.1884, with Canning Street crossing left to right. Below is a later view from the south-west, with the entrance to Spring Street on the left, marked by the former Providence Inn on the corner. St Stephen's was damaged during the Second World War, and as demolition began in 1955, pleas to preserve the remaining 180 foot tower and spire were rejected – the council unwilling to spend the £15,000 necessary to restore it. The site was cleared by April 1956, and is now completely lost beneath the retail and leisure complex, which retains the name St Stephen's.

119 1929.317 (11.5 x 15.2 cm) above
Named after the chairman of the Hull School Board, Thomas Stratten School was opened in 1881. Situated on the south side of Londesborough Street, it had initial accommodation for 797 children. Closing in 1969, it was then used as an annexe of Hull College in the 1980s, and demolished in 2000.

120 1929.235 (13.8 x 10.3 cm) left New Rifle Barracks were built for the Hull Volunteer Rifle Corps, designed by architect Ensign R A Marillier, with work commencing in February 1864. The site belonged partly to the North Eastern Railway Co, and partly to Miss Broadley, and was situated at the rear of Thanet House in Park Street (presently part of the Hull College). Initially access was only through the private grounds of the house – then the home of Rev H W Kemp – chaplain to the Corps. First known as the Park Street Barracks, the facility was partially opened in July 1864, but completion was delayed by a brick-layers strike until the October. The construction of the barracks was the impetus for the re-naming of the lane, as Londesborough Street in 1864, after Lord Londesborough – honorary colonel of the First East Yorkshire Rifle Volunteers. Smith's view looks west from Park Street, c.1885; the barracks survive in part, and are just visible on the left, before the school.

121 1929.203 (13.2 x 18.8 cm) This is the opposite view of Londesborough Street to that shown on page 92. The old track that was to become Londesborough Street, originally ran along the line of the Myton Carr Sewer, which served as a natural boundary – dividing ownership of the land to its north and south.
This track along the bank of the old sewer or dyke, gave access to the Asylum, Asylum Lane, and pleasure gardens either side of West Parade. Laid out in the early 1800s, West Parade initially ran north from the Anlaby Road in a direct line through to the dyke, but was divided by the arrival of the railway in 1846.
This west end of Londesborough Street was widened, and developed a gradient,

due to the construction of a raised approach to the Argyle Street road bridge. The bridge was built over the North Eastern Railway's lines in 1886 (just off the right hand side of this picture – see following page). Smith's drawing, dated 1888, shows the scene just after the bridge construction works, with new walls and fences in place, and with a large area to the north side (left) of the street that was developed with housing and shops just months later.
Most of the original buildings in Londesborough Street were demolished from the mid-1970s, and now only the barracks, the Clarendon pub, a small terrace of shops, and a terrace of private housing remain.

122 1929.365 (13.1 x 19 cm) Almost certainly drawn at the same time as the previous drawing, this shows the view looking south, from the top of the Argyle Street road bridge over the railway lines in 1888. A 'new street from Derringham Street to Argyle Street' was proposed as part of the Town Improvement Schemes from 1884. The development of this new link road, caused the re-development of the west end of Londesborough Street, the extension of Argyle Street – north to join Derringham Street, and the construction of a road bridge, replacing the level-crossing in Argyle Street. The road bridge was constructed in 1887, at a predicted cost of around £6,500.

Looking south towards the Anlaby Road, the series of buildings on left were associated with the Hull Workhouse of 1852 – the site of Hull Royal Infirmary since 1966-67. The entrance through the wall gave access to a convalescent ward and hospital, at the rear of the workhouse, which is the building with the pedimented gable on the far left. At the time of writing, part of the original convalescent ward, and a block of property built in the 1920s as an extension to the hospital (latterly used as nurses accommodation), remain in use by the modern infirmary. All of the property on the right-hand side of Argyle Street in this view, was demolished from 1972 onwards, and gone by the 1990s.

Sponsored by Malcolm Shields

123 1929.128 (11.2 x 15.5 cm) This drawing looks west along the Anlaby Road c.1887. The tall ornate building on the immediate left, was The Circus, established here by Charles Hengler in 1864 as 'The Grand Cirque Variete'. This remained as a popular dance venue, latterly known as The Palace, until demolition in 1966. Beyond the theatre and the short terrace of shops, Smith depicts a group of carriages around the junction of Great Thornton Street (left) and Park Street, off the picture on the right. Further west, beyond the entrance to Great Thornton Street, was the housing of Coburg Terrace, beyond which can be seen the roof and spire of the Wycliffe Chapel, built in 1867-68.

All of the buildings on the left – the south side of the road – were demolished from the Second World War onwards, and the view is now dominated by blocks of flats, built during the redevelopment of the area in the 1960s and 1970s. On the right of the picture, are a series of ramshackle properties that extended from the entrance to Paragon Station, westwards all the way to the Park Street entrance. Some dated from the 1840s, and were associated with roperies and other small industries, established along the undeveloped north side of the Anlaby Road. Many of the small shacks were eventually replaced with more substantial buildings, a small number of which, remain in use today.

124 1929.206 (13.5 x 19.3 cm) Looking east towards the city centre, this 1889 drawing looks back to the point at which the last drawing ended. On the far left is the entrance to Lansdowne Street, laid out in 1861, which now forms part of the entrance to the Hull Royal Infirmary. The three large houses leading to the corner formed West Parade Terrace – taking its name from the long-established West Parade, at the east end of the terrace. The corner property on the extreme left, was known as Lansdowne House. This was a boarding house and hotel from c.1915 until the 1940s, and in the 1960s was converted for use as a Nurses Home, for the newly built infirmary. Having out-lived its neighbours in the short terrace by a decade or more, it was badly damaged in a fire in 1976, and demolished. Directly opposite West Parade Terrace, can be seen one half of a charity refuge

established in March 1811. Known as Hope House, it was described in the minutes of a Guildhall meeting that year as: a 'place of reception for those unhappy women, who having followed vicious courses, may be desirous of obtaining the means of reformation'. The property Smith shows was a rebuilt property of c.1837, which was demolished in the 1970s. Beyond Hope House is a long old, low property, known as Carr Cottage; this was associated with a windmill established c.1807, later converted to an oil mill known as Carr's Mill. Behind Carr Cottage can be seen a building that was built on the site of a private residence known as Myton House; the 'Roman Catholic Convent and School of the Sisters of Mercy' was founded here in 1857. Both convent and school were damaged in the Second World War, and demolished in 1954.

125 1929.160 (11.7 x 16.1 cm) right Hull's Botanic Gardens were established on a site south of the Anlaby Road in 1811. Inspired by the gardens in Liverpool, Hull's were only the third of that kind in England, and opened to subscribers in June 1812. The lane leading to the site was named Botanic Lane, but re-named Linnaeus Street c.1823, after the Swedish botanist Carl Linnaeus. As the gardens became surrounded by housing and industry, and the accompanying smoke and smells, the gardens lost a lot of support; allowing only subscribers to use the gardens also greatly effected profits. In 1877 the decision was made to remove the gardens to a setting that allowed them to expand, and add more attractions, as they had made a large loss in the previous years. Land was purchased from the North Eastern Railway, south of what we know as Spring Bank West, at around £700 per acre, and in 1879 the old site was sold. The new gardens, of over 55 acres, opened in July 1880; Smith's drawing is of c.1888, looking south with the spire of St Matthew's church on the Anlaby Road in the distance.

By 1886 the Botanic Gardens were again in debt, and in 1887 part of the site was sold to the Hull Football Club, the balance used for the creation of Hymers College, which opened in 1893.

126 1981.415.84 (12.7 x 17.5 cm) left In 1882 advertisements appeared for: 'land suitable for a west park'. Prospective sites were, amongst others, land at the Botanic Gardens, and another with 76 acres of land and a frontage to Mill Lane, at the south-west end of the Anlaby Road. However, a 50-acre site on the north side of the Anlaby Road was chosen, which the corporation had purchased from the North Eastern Railway Company in 1878. In 1884 it was agreed that the land should be drained and 'thrown open to the public – with steps taken at once to use the site as a public park'. An initial suggestion for the park's name was Albert Park, but that was rejected by the Parks Committee. Borough Engineer Mr J Fox Sharpe designed the park, and the cost of its construction was estimated at just over £13,000 'including all the requisite buildings, bridges etc'. Sir A K Rollit opened the new 'Western District Park' on 29 August 1885, when the Hull Critic newspaper described the Park as: 'the formation of an additional lung for the many thousands of inhabitants with which the west end of the town is populated'. Smith's sketch of the park dates from c.1886, looking south towards the Anlaby Road.

127 1929.290 (21.3 x 14.2 cm) The 'Wold Carr Toll Bar' on the Anlaby Turnpike Road, was situated east of the line of Walton Street, at a point that marked the municipal boundary (until extension in 1882); the tolls were abolished in 1873, and the gates removed. The site of the toll-bar, and toll-bar gate-keeper's house was built upon c.1873, with Cumberland Terrace – four three-storey, purpose-built shops, with accommodation above. The first occupants were grocer George Shaw, draper Samuel Rowe, boot manufacturer John Rodhouse and confectioner Henry Bell. When the KC Stadium opened in 2002, this east side of the Walton Street entrance was widened to accommodate the increased traffic, and what remained of Cumberland Terrace was demolished in 2003.

Also visible on the far left of this 1892 drawing, is a pub that was established long before Cumberland Terrace was built. The Wold Carr Inn was built c.1860,

and was recorded in the 1861 Census. It is likely that inn was used as a works office, for the building sites north of the Anlaby Road in the 1860s, as was the Brickmaker's Arms in Walton Street. Pubs were often the first properties to be built in developments, and even before they were licensed, were used as make-shift works offices, and rooms for workers to shelter and receive their wages. Shown here with its original three-storeys, the top floor was removed after the Second World War, probably as a safety measure following bomb damage.

A long-standing Moors' & Robson's pub, it was known as the Newington Inn from 1876. From c.1901 until the early 1930s, the pub was run by the Parker family – notably Ernest Parker, who also had a local fruit and vegetable shop. Thus the colloquial name 'Parker's' has been associated with the pub ever since, and was officially adopted in recent years.

Sponsored by Wendy Loncaster

128 1981.415.60 (12.5 x 17.5 cm) Somerset House (or Villa) was a large detached property, built c.1861 for Hull businessman William Norman, late of Hessle. Mr Norman established his business as a tailor, draper, hatter and outfitter, in Humber Street c.1840, and had premises in Queen Street when he retired c.1860 (the 1861 Census records him as retired, and living at an address in Hessle). Set back from the Anlaby Road in its own grounds, the house had formal gardens front and rear, that were adjoined by large stables.

A small cottage was built at the east side of the house, adjoining the stable block and coach house, and became known as Norman's Cottage. The 1881 Census listed William Norman as a retired tailor and outfitter, aged 66 years, with his wife Elizabeth aged 44, and two servants also living at the large house. According to the Census, Norman's Cottage was occupied by the Norman's gardener – Joseph Shields, aged 53, with his wife Emma, three children, and a grandson.

Somerset House was also known locally as Peace & Plenty House, when first built, in reference to two statues that originally stood in the alcoves, either side of the building.

By 1905 only Mrs Norman was listed at Somerset House, and in 1910 it was demolished for the construction of the Wenlock Territorial Army Barracks, which opened in 1911. Just one age-worn stone gate post survives, as a reminder of the former Somerset House, at the end of a wall next to the Beetonsville Post Office.

129 1981.415.62 (15 x 18.5 cm) right, and 130 1981.415.61 (15 x 19 cm) below On the south side of the Anlaby Road, opposite Cumberland Terrace, was Maiden Hill Farm. The term 'Maydnhill' is mentioned in documents dating from 1482, although the property Smith recorded in these 1894 drawings was probably of a later date – most-likely 18th Century.

Latterly home to well-known farmer Samuel Beecroft, until his death in 1861, the house shown here from the Anlaby Road frontage (below) and from the south (right) was Maiden Hill House, adjacent to a series of farm building set to its west. Following Beecroft's death, the household and furniture was described in a sale notice in the Hull Packet as: 'Sitting-room, Four Lodging rooms, Two Kitchens, an excellent Summer or Greenhouse, an Arbour, one 3-light and one 2-light Hot-bed Frames, sundry Tools & etc., together with Four prime HAMS and Four sides of BACON, home fed.'

Maiden Hill Farm was demolished in the late 1890s – hence Smith's drawings, created as a record of the historic buildings. The present Perry Street, Ruskin Street and Walliker Street were built upon the former farm, which at that time extended to around two and a half acres.

131 1929.473 (22.5 x 27.3 cm) above, and 132
1929.182 (12 x 8.9 cm) left Coltman Street took its
name from the Coltman family, who owned the land
on which it was built. The Reverend Joseph Coltman
of Beverley, left the land to his son – Sir Thomas
Coltman, who named the street in honour of his
father, who died in 1837. The street developed slowly
from c.1845, from the Hessle Road end, joining with
an older alignment off the south side of Anlaby Road.
Coltman Street is mentioned in the local press from
1845, and was listed in trade directories from 1846,
but the slow development was cause for concern
as late as 1849. A speaker at a meeting of the Myton
Commissioners in that year, noted that: '671 yards of
the street were built upon, and 1,125 were unbuilt;
the total frontage being 1,796 yards, and the street
is neither paved nor flagged'. He also commented
that: 'Coltman Street was a disgrace to the town ...
if a stranger were to enter the town by either the
Anlaby Road or Hessle Road, and wished to pass from
one of those roads to the other, he would find the
thoroughfare in a clayey state and all but impassable'.
The surviving original properties, particularly those at
the far north (shown above) and far south (left), are a
clear reminder of a typical c.1850 suburban Hull street.

133 1929.307 (13.1 x 18.8 cm) left Daltry Street was one of several new streets, laid-out off the 'new' Hessle Road in the late 1860s. Sir Henry Cooper laid the foundation stone of the Daltry Street Board School, on Monday 24 February 1873, and it was notable as the first new school to be built by the Hull School Board. Daltry Street School cost £4,497 to construct, and the site was purchased for £1,722; it provided places for an initial 760 children in three departments, later increased to 1,020 with the addition of a junior department in 1896.

At the time the school opened, the Hull School Board had a deficiency of 7,000 places in the town; temporary places had been found for 2,600, and many more new schools were built in the next decade.

The School Boards were abolished by the Balfour Education Act of 1902, which replaced them with around 300 Local Education Authorities; by that time Hull had around 40 Board Schools, with over 33,000 places.

Seen here in 1889, Daltry Street's departments closed one by one from 1927, and suffered Blitz damage in 1942. The school was demolished in the 1960s.

134 1929.303 (13.2 x 19 cm) right
Also drawn by Smith in 1889, was the newly-built West Dock Avenue Board School, shown here from the west side of the street. The school opened in 1888, and was typical of the large schools built at that time, with accommodation for 876 pupils in three departments.

Similar to Daltry Street, an extra junior department was added in 1898, and by the turn of the century there were places for 1,221 pupils. The school was re-organised several times, and by 1935 had places for 310 senior boys, 264 junior boys, and 319 infants; in 1945 the senior boys became known as St Andrew's High School, which continued until 1967, when most of the housing in this area was demolished. The large old school complex, which stretched through to Harrow Street, was demolished in 1985-86.

135 1995.27 (21 x 25 cm) left The 'Hull Bank for Savings' was formed following an Act of Parliament, which set regulations for the operation of Savings Banks throughout the United Kingdom, in conjunction with the Bank of England. Hull's first branch was opened on 3 January 1818, when a report in the press noted, that its design and object was to: 'encourage the labouring classes and others to deposit a portion of their earnings, however small, (not less than one shilling at a time) as suits their convenience'.

Between opening and 17 February almost £7,000 was paid-in to Hull's first branch, and by the end of the first year gross deposits were over £32,000. A secretary for the bank was employed in 1819, at a salary of £100 per annum, the first regular branch being situated in Exchange Alley. In 1829 a purpose-built bank, designed by local architect George Jackson junior of Princess Street, was built in Posterngate – adjoining the hospital of the Trinity House.

The 'West End' branch of the Hull Savings Bank, was the first to open outside the city centre. Built on the corner of Neptune Street, at no.89 Hessle Road, it was drawn by Smith just after opening in 1893.

136 1929.244 (13.5 x 19.3 cm) right Further west along the Hessle Road, at the corner of Boulevard, was St Barnabas Church. The foundation stone of the church was laid in June 1872, and it was consecrated in February 1874. Built on a site of 1,265 square yards, donated by Mr Henry Strickland Constable of Hornsea, the church was designed by Samuel Musgrave, in the Early English style, and had seating for over 700. It cost around £4,000 to build, and the contractors were Benjamin Musgrave & Sons. Shown here in 1888, looking east along the Hessle Road, the church closed in 1970, and was soon demolished; the site is now occupied by housing.

137 1981.415.64 (15.3 x 22.2 cm) The Rose Tavern was established c.1863, at the north end of Alfred Street (no.2), as a licensed Ale & Porter Store. It was first run by Dennis Taylor, who was also the long-standing licensee of the Sheffield Arms, on the Hessle Road. By 1867 the pub was also listed as no.37 Hessle Road, as it was the corner property, and the 'tavern' – actually a licensed beer-house – was recorded by name as the Rose Tavern in the 1871 Census. Mrs Elizabeth Branton was listed as the beer-house keeper and head of the household in the census, as her husband Charles – the previous keeper – had died in 1870.

Also at the property, still recorded as no.2 Alfred Street, were her two sons John and William, both scholars. Mr Charles Hart, a stone-mason by trade, was also listed as a boarder, and from 1872 Mr Hart was listed in trade directories as the

licensee of the Rose Tavern. Tate's Brewery of Lime Street in the Groves, owned the Rose, from the 1880s, and when the company was acquired by the Hull Brewery Co in 1896, the Rose was rebuilt; the rebuilding was recorded in the Town Improvement Committee Minutes in 1896. An advertisement for John Tate's Mild Ales can be seen on the wall of the pub, and John Tate became a director of the Hull Brewery.

It seems certain that the date of Smith's drawing was 1896, and that he was recording the loss of the old pub. The new building was of three-storeys, with Dutch gables, and was itself demolished c.1969-70 under a Compulsory Purchase Order for the area, which also saw the demolition of two more old Hessle Road pubs – the nearby Lily Hotel, and Foundry Arms.

138 1981.415.68 (13.2 x 16.5 cm) Smith made this sketch in 1892, at a point where five roads once converged. Smith was standing at the end of Walker Street looking south, with the entrance to Porter Street and Waverley Street on his left. Walker Street was named after James Walker of Beverley, who owned the land on which this area was developed in the late 1830s. Directly opposite was St James Street (originally known as Cent-Per-Cent Street), with the tower of St James Church visible over the rooftops on the left. On his right was the point at which the Hessle Road began, marked by the Vauxhall Tavern at no.1 Hessle Road, as it still is today. The Vauxhall Tavern was established in 1825 – as the Hessle Road as we know it was being developed – and is the only building that survives from this scene in 2011. A turnpike road to Hessle was planned from 1824, and prior to this the main road here was known as Patrick Ground Lane. After the turnpike road was opened in 1825, that part of Patrick Ground Lane east of this junction became Waverley Street, and west of this junction became Hessle Road. Demolition in the area began in the 1950s, and continued sporadically until Clive Sullivan Way, swept through west Hull in the 1980s.

Sponsored by Geoff Percival

139 1981.415.65 (15.4 x 11.4 cm) This sketch shows Lister Street looking west towards St James Church, and dates from c.1885. The street was laid-out in 1829, on land that had formerly housed pleasure and market gardens. This was part of a development sited around a new church for South Myton – St James, which opened in 1831 – and can be seen dominating the west end of the street. As this was a developing area, many of the initial residents reflected the needs of the building trades. In 1842, when the street was still only half-built upon, residents included a public works contractor, a gas contractor, a slate merchant, and a civil engineer, as well as three priests, and several merchants, councillors and solicitors.

No.36 Lister Street was sold in 1836, and the sale notice described the substantial property as:
'... a newly-erected Dwelling House, containing on the Ground Floor, a Breakfast Room 16 by 14 feet, a Dining Room 18 by 16 feet, Two Lodging Rooms each 16 by 14, one of them communicating with a Dressing Room. Three other good Lodging Rooms, and a Water Closet on the Landing. There is also a Nursery, Store Rooms, and other conveniences, and an excellent Wine Cellar. There are Two dry Cellar Kitchens, each 16 by 14 feet, and a large lead Cistern, also a large Reservoir in the yard.

The Garden is spacious, is walled around, and well Stocked with the choicest Apricot, Nectarine, and other Fruit Trees, and the Walks are all Flagged.

The Ground Plot of this Property contains about 340 Square Yards. This House was built by the Owner, for his own residence, and no expense has been spared to finish it in the best style, for comfort and sustainability; the Neighbourhood is Respectable and Airy'.

The residents were clearly of the upper classes – note the mounting blocks in street, indicating that houses could afford horse transport – in stark contrast to the mostly working class houses that filled the surrounding area, many of which could only be described as slums.

Lister Street's houses were mostly demolished under a 1963 Compulsory Purchase Order, by which time most of the larger houses shown in Smith's sketch had been converted to flats. The street is now little more than an access road, in an industrial and retail area, with no surviving original buildings.

Thank you

 A D R Sound Sense, sound and video production, www.adrsoundsense.com

Susan Capes, Assistant Curator – Projects – Hull Museums for assistance, and permission to reproduce the Smith drawings

Rob Barnard for proof reading and support

East Yorkshire Local History Society (K.A. MacMahon Fund)

Ian Halstead for layout and design advice, and proof-reading

Martin Hayes, County Local Studies Librarian, Worthing Library in Sussex, for the two images of Worthing used in the introduction (page 4), and for assistance in researching Smith's family details in Worthing

Hull Maritime Society, with particular thanks to Arthur Credland

Wendy Loncaster

Pat Nendick for genealogical assistance

Geoff Percival

Caroline Rhodes, Collections Curator, Hull Museums

Malcolm Shields

Martin Taylor – the City Archivist, and the staff of the Hull History Centre, for permission to reproduce the following images: Rose Street in 1971 (THD.3.193.36 on page 5), Eastbourne Avenue in 1940 (TSP.4.290.6 on page 6), and Eastbourne Avenue 1972 (THD.3.214.8a, also page 6)

Gail and **Lily**, for their continuing encouragement and entertainment

FSC
MIX
Paper from responsible sources
FSC® C022612
www.fsc.org

F. S. Smith's Hull – Then and Now

An Exhibition at the Hull Maritime Museum

9 May 2011 – 11 September 2011

This exhibition features some of F. S. Smith's original drawings of Victorian Hull and its suburbs, many previously unseen. It reveals how much Hull has changed, by comparing Smith's drawings, with photographs of the same views today

As well as exploring changes to our City through events such as the Second World War, urban regeneration, and the expansion of Hull's suburban housing, Victorian ways of life – often highlighted in minute detail in Smith's drawings – will be reflected in displays of related objects, from the Hull Museums collections

We are endeavouring to raise funds, towards the conservation and preservation of this important and unique collection, within Hull Museums. If you would like to make a donation – however small – please contact Hull Museums:

Hull Museums
Monument Buildings
Queen Victoria Square
Hull   HU1 3RA

01482 – 613902
museums@hullcc.gov.uk

Brief Bibliography

Lost Churches and Chapels of Hull. David Neave, with Geoff Bell, Christopher Ketchell and Susan Neave, Hull City Museums & Art Galleries and the Hutton Press. Cherry Burton, 1991

Victoria County History of the County of York and the East Riding. Volume 1. The City of Kingston upon Hull. Edited by K.J. Allison, Oxford University Press for the Institute of Historical Research. 1969

Hull Pubs & Breweries. Paul Gibson, Tempus Publishing Ltd. Stroud, 2004

Holderness Road, Through the Heart of East Hull. Mary Fowler, Highgate Publications (Beverley) Ltd. Beverley, 1990

The Buildings of England. Yorkshire: York and the East Riding. Nikolaus Pevsner and David Neave, Penguin Books. 1972 (second edition 1995)

History of the Streets of Hull. J Richardson, a Malet Lambert re-print of an original series of articles in the East Yorkshire Times in 1915. Hull, 1980

Architecture of the Victorian Era of Kingston upon Hull; Being a Study of the Principal Buildings Erected in Hull, 1830-1914. Ian N. Goldthorpe (edited by Margaret Sumner), Highgate Publications (Beverley) Ltd. Beverley, 2005

A New Picture of Georgian Hull. Ivan and Elizabeth Hall, William Sessions Ltd, York and Hull Civic Society. Hull, 1978

Hull in the Eighteenth Century, a Study in Economic and Social History. Gordon Jackson, Oxford University Press. 1972

History of the Town & Port of Kingston upon Hull. John James Sheahan, John Green. Beverley, 1862

Hull In The 1950s: A Pictorial Diary of Life in Kingston upon Hull. John E. Smith, Hutton Press Ltd. Cherry Burton, 1994

Landlord. Graham Wilkinson, unpublished. Hull, 2007

Tremendous Activity in the Old Town; Demolitions Loss List 1943-1988. Chris Ketchell, Hull College Local History Unit. Hull, 1989

The Anlaby Road. Paul Gibson, Friends of Lonsdale Community Centre. Hull, 2007

Lost Pubs of Hull. Paul Gibson & Graham Wilkinson, Kingston Press. Hull, 1999

The History of Spring Bank, 'A Pleasant and Beautiful Promenade'. Chris Ketchell, Hull College Local History Unit. Hull, 1996

Spring Bank, This Pleasing Suburban Road. Chris Ketchell, Hull College Local History Unit. Hull, 1997

The Beverley Road Walk, A Noble Approach to the Town. Chris Ketchell, Hull College Local History Unit. Hull, 1997

Thirteen Bridges Trail. Chris Ketchell, Hull College Local History Unit. Hull, 1996

Illustrated Guide to Hull. Edmund Wrigglesworth, Brown & Sons. Hull, 1890

Moors' & Robson's Breweries Ltd. A Brief History. Rob Barnard, Hull College Local History Unit. Hull, 1996

Trinity House of Kingston upon Hull. Arthur Storey, Albert Gait Ltd Grimsby, 1967

140 1929.354 (15.7 x 11.3 cm) This door originally led into one of Hull's first prisons in Fetter Lane – latterly used as part of Samuel Beecroft's basket-making business. Smith was recording the former House of Correction – later used as a lock-up – just before it was demolished in 1884. See map on page 42.

Evidences Relating to the Eastern Part of the City of Kingston upon Hull.
Thomas Blashill, A Brown & Sons. Hull, 1903

Hull Camera 1964-1991. A Photographer's View of Hull. Ted Tuxworth, Hutton Press. Cherry Burton, 1991

Cotton Manufacture in Kingston upon Hull. Reprinted from Business History Vol.IV, No.2, June 1962. Joyce M. Bellamy, Liverpool University Press. Liverpool, 1962

Hull School Board Schools. Information sheet. Chris Ketchell, Hull College Local History Unit. Hull, 2001

Hull Museums Publications, No.165. Catalogue of the Fewster Collection of F S Smith's Sketches of Old Hull. Thomas Sheppard, The Museum. Hull, 1929

Images of Victorian Hull. F S Smith's Drawings of the Old Town. Carolyn Aldridge, Hull City Museums & Art Galleries and Hutton Press. Cherry Burton, 1989

F S Smith's Drawings of Hull. Images of 'Victorian' Hull 2. Christopher Ketchell, in association with Hull City Museums & Art Galleries. Hull City Museums & Art Galleries and the Hutton Press. Cherry Burton, 1990

Hull and East Riding Breweries. From the Eighteenth Century to the Present. Pat Aldabella and Rob Barnard, East Yorkshire Local History Society. Hull, 1997

City of Kingston upon Hull. Calendar of the Ancient Deeds, Letters, Miscellaneous Old Documents, &c., in the Archives of the Corporation. L.M. Stanwell, Guildhall. Hull, 1951

Artists and Craftsmen of Hull and East Yorkshire. Arthur Credland, Hull Museums and Art Gallery. Hull, 2000

Excavations in Sewer Lane, Hull 1974. East Riding Archaeologist Vol.3 1977, Hull Old Town Report Series No.1. Peter Armstrong, East Riding Archaeological Society. Hull, 1977

Hull Then & Now 2, Another Look at Hull's Heritage. Paul Gibson, Carnegie Heritage Centre. Hull, 2010

House of Commons Accounts & Papers, Nine Volumes Relating to Corporate Offices and Charitable Funds, Vol.XLV. House of Commons,1834

The History of Reckitt & Sons Limited. Basil N. Reckitt, A Brown & Sons. Hull, 1952

Inns of Holderness and Taverns of East Hull. John Wilson Smith (edited by Rob Barnard). Hull College Local History Unit. Hull, 1996

British Listed Buildings. www.britishlistedbuildings.co.uk

19th Century British Newspapers: Hull Packet. Hull City Council Leisure & Culture on-line resource

Bank of England Archive. www.bankofengland.co.uk/about/history/archive

United Kingdom Census Returns. www.ancestry.co.uk

United Kingdom Census Returns. www.findmypast.co.uk

Trade Directories (various). Author's collection

Google Earth. www.google.co.uk/intl/en_uk/earth

141 1929.352 (12.8 x 9.1 cm) right Hull's former Citadel was demolished in 1863-64, but this 17th Century stone watch tower – called a Bartizan, survived. It was displayed in the East Park for many years, but has more recently been re-located within the Victoria Dock Estate. See map on page 42.

142 1929.395 (13.5 x 19 cm) Smith made this sketch looking north along the River Hull, from Sculcoates Bridge. Dated December 1889, it shows the heart of industrial Hull. On the left, the seed-crushing mills of Eyre & Co., and John Ellershaw, both based in Church Street (Wincolmlee), and on the right the seed-crushing mill of David Salmond & Co, and the varnish, paint & whiting manufactory of John W Davis & Son, both situated off Stoneferry Road in Wilmington. See map on page 22.